JAMES BOYCE IS LATE

This book has received financial assistance under the Cultural Traditions Programme which aims to encourage acceptance and understanding of cultural diversity.

The Friar's Bush Press
24 College Park Avenue
BELFAST BT7 1LR
Published 1990
© Copyright reserved
ISBN 0 946872 33 3

Front cover painted by Barbara Allen.
Printed by W. & G. Baird, Antrim.

JAMES BOYCE IS LATE

A Country Schoolroom and Beyond

by

JACK CLAYPOLE

FRIAR'S BUSH PRESS

CONTENTS

TO MY WIFE

INTRODUCTION

Shortly after the War I was, for nearly three years, the principal teacher of a two-teacher school in a remote part of County Fermanagh, Northern Ireland, and this book is based upon my experiences during that time. All the events and people are described according to my memories of them, but I have used fictitious names for all the characters, and for all the places, except for major towns such as Belfast and Enniskillen. Nevertheless they are all real people and real places, especially Kinowla Public Elementary School, which is the centre of these reminiscences. The conversations of course, are invented, and I have not attempted to reproduce the sounds of Fermanagh voices, although a former pupil volunteered to act as my language consultant!

I had lived all my life in Bristol, where I was involved in youth work and worked in an office until joining the R. A. F. , but I was trained as a teacher at Larkfield Training College near Belfast, since I was offered a place there on the day after my demobilisation. My wife comes from Belfast, and it was therefore a new experience for both of us to live in the heart of the country, in a cottage without electricity and water. It was strange for me to spend my first years of teaching in a school of a kind of which I was totally unaware before becoming its principal. But those early days, so unfamiliar at first and now so distant, are etched sharply upon my mind, and I recall them with pleasure and affection, feelings which, I hope, will be clear to all who read about them.

If Sir Edward Elgar had not already used the phrase to preface the score of his 'Enigma Variations,' I would have dedicated this book 'to my friends pictured within,' all of whom I remember so fondly and so well. Without them the book would not have been possible; without the constant help and encouragement of my wife it would not have been written. I am indeed grateful to her, and to all the children and people of Kinowla, who welcomed us among them, and made us so happy there.

Jack Claypole

1   *James Boyce is Late*

EACH DAY the end seat had been empty. I rang the bell and the children trooped into the high-ceilinged schoolroom and sat at the long, backless desks, but always the seat at the right of the front desk was left unoccupied as if waiting to be filled by someone, who was always expected but never came. There was a lonely air about it, but by the time school ended, the empty seat appeared normal, a space that remained unoccupied, yet some day would be filled like the others.

But now, on a bright wintry morning, at last it was filled, for there, sitting in the hitherto vacant seat, was a tall boy with cropped black hair, whose round face contrasted starkly with his gaunt body. His cheeks were pale, and the eyes were sunken and dark, yet his face was brightened by a huge, water-melon grin. Whoever he was, this boy did not look well cared for; his clothes were too small for his angular frame, his wrists stuck out from the ragged cuffs of his shabby jacket, and the frayed edges of his trousers ended far above his muddy boots, which projected beyond the iron legs of the desk.

As I had done each day since becoming Principal of Kinowla Public Elementary School just one week earlier, I wished the children 'Good morning,' opened the register and began to call the roll. 'James Boyce?' I said, and made to move on without waiting for an answer, for as yet, there had never been one; but before I could do so, a voice loud enough to make up for all the days when its owner had not been present to reply, called 'Yes sir!' and the newcomer's face expanded into an immense beam, his smile became even wider and his black hair changed to a dark halo of pure pleasure, surrounding the white glow of his face. So this was the mysterious James Boyce, and even at this first encounter, I could tell that he was no

1

ordinary boy. I had heard about James's older brother Ernie, who had now left school, if indeed he could ever have been said to have started, for his attendance had been uncommon and irregular. On Ernie's first day at school, at some undefined age, but well above that for compulsory education, he had entered that same schoolroom wearing a trilby hat, which he had resolutely refused to remove, stating loudly and defiantly that he always wore his hat, and would not come to school without it. Ernie Boyce was a big lad, and the teacher was a small lady, so the trilby stayed on Ernie's head all that day and all the other days, few though they were, when Ernie, for reasons best known to himself, deigned to appear at school.

Both he and James looked neglected; their mother was a mystery as far as the school was concerned, and their father even more so, but it was considered prudent not to enquire too deeply into the family, or into the reasons for any of its activities, and certainly, the School Attendance Officer never did so! James was now 13 years old according to the register, but he had started school so late, and had then come so rarely, that he had been placed in the front row with the children aged eight. As I was to find out, even that was entirely by courtesy, for his educational achievements were little better than those of the year's new entrants, but he did not seem to mind where he sat, and after all, there was more room for his legs at the front. As far as I could tell, James was unaware of his disadvantages, and happiness continued to illuminate his presence throughout the calling of the remaining names on the register, and the general bustle of commencing work for the day.

My class of about 22 boys and girls aged from 8-14, was divided into two groups, roughly according to age, and I asked the younger children and James, to carry on with some handwriting practice from their copy-books, whilst I sat at the end of the desk behind them, and began to discuss the events of the week-end with the older group. Gradually I became aware of an undercurrent of tittering and giggling behind me, which was unusual, so I turned round and saw Pauline Taylor, a nine-year-old girl, with long, straggling, reddish hair, grinning broadly, and waving her hand frantically in the air.

'What's wrong, Pauline?' I asked, but she could only splutter in reply.

'Pauline!' I demanded. 'What's the matter with you?' She did her best to control herself and finally managed to say, 'It's not me, it's James Boyce!' before dissolving into laughter once more.

'Well, what about James Boyce? What's wrong with him?' More splutters followed. 'Please. . . please. . . he can't write; well, only his name!'

This was something I had not expected. No college lecturer had mentioned 13 year-olds who couldn't write, and the thought had never crossed my mind. I went to James and saw that his page was clean and unmarked. He smiled as I spoke to him. 'James,' I said, 'can you copy the words in that book?' Another big smile and he replied, 'No, but I can write my name,' and a feeling of pride shone through the words. By now the laughter had died down, and I was aware that work had stopped; the children were looking at James and myself, wondering what I would do, for was I not the new 'Master,' fresh from college, and an Englishman too? 'That's fine, James,' I replied 'Will you please write your name in the book for me?' He nodded happily, put his tongue between his teeth, picked up his pencil, and with tremendous effort and concentration, slowly and painfully he wrote, in reasonably well formed letters, 'James Boyce is late'. Then he looked up at me with an expression of pride and satisfaction. 'What does it say?' I asked him. Obviously puzzled, he answered, 'James Boyce, that's my name.' and he read aloud, 'James Boyce,' pointing at the words as he did so, but underlining all four of them in the process.

Now we were both baffled, so I asked him to write his name again, and once more he wrote, 'James Boyce is late,' evidently thinking that he had written his name and nothing else. After such a long delay, the other children were losing interest, and most had resumed work, but the older ones were waiting for my attention. However, I was wondering what to do about James's inability to decipher his own name, and then recalled that we had been told always to praise effort, so praise James I did. 'Well done James,' I said in my most encouraging voice, 'that's very good indeed. I'll talk to you about it later. Now just take out a book and go on reading. You know where to find a book don't you?'

This provoked the biggest outburst of my one week long teaching career. The entire class erupted in a vast gale of laughter, the first real emotion they had shown so far, and I could not understand the reason for it; the reception given to my best jokes had been only lukewarm, yet here was true laughter, although no-one had said or done anything funny. As usual Pauline was the cheer-leader; she was shaking like a be-spectacled jelly, her hair was waving and her eyes dancing with merriment.

'Well Pauline,' I asked, beginning to feel a little rattled, 'is it James Boyce this time?' She could barely answer but nodded her head, and at last blurted out, 'Yes! He can't read either!' and at this she and all the others laughed even more loudly. Only then did I realise that the joke was on me: how could I have been so stupid as to ask James to read, when it should have been clear that he was unable to do so. Luckily I had sense enough to see the funny side of the matter, and to join in with the children and with James himself, who was bubbling with glee, determined to have his share of the fun, of which he had been the unwitting cause. The children were laughing at me and not at James, they were amused by my foolish reaction to an unexpected situation, and by my fall from grace; I learned later that they never laughed at anyone's lack of ability, for that would have been foreign to their kind and gentle natures, but when the Master did something silly, that was a different matter. I realised too, that even the best of training could not prepare one for all eventualities, even in such an uneventful school as Kinowla appeared to be.

We managed to settle down at last, and I asked David Reed, who was sitting next to James, to keep an eye upon him; an ironic choice, for David was a younger and smaller boy, who had hardly any more skill than James, but he accepted his duties gracefully, and peace was restored. But not for long. Soon I was aware of a tall figure standing beside me, and James's voice asked, 'Please can I make up the fire?' The school was heated, (in theory!) by a black, coal-burning range, and as there was no caretaker, the principal had to clean it out and light the fire each morning, and then keep it burning all day . . . there had been no lectures on stoking at college either! Anxious to ensure that James was usefully occupied, I readily agreed, a decision made lightly then; I had never heard of safety regulations and fire precautions at that time. Still the fact that the fire was unguarded shows that I was not alone in disregarding such perils, for obviously the school had never had a fireguard, and I must add that, although I taught for many years in rooms with such dangerous fires, no accident ever took place.

Despite any possible danger, it was the best decision I could have made. James left, and I thought no more about him until it was time for me to speak to his group, and then I noticed how brightly the fire was burning, how clean the hearth was, and saw a pile of chopped sticks propped up nearby. Only then did I become aware of James's absence, but before I could comment, the door opened and in he walked, carrying more sticks, which he placed neatly alongside the others, taking care that none fell as he did so. Giving me a huge smile, James lifted the lid of the range, ensured that the fire was burning well, replaced the lid, and returning to his seat, folded his arms and beamed yet again.

'Where did you get those sticks, James?' I enquired, remembering that there had been none left in the fuel shed after I had lit the fire that morning. 'I chopped them,' he replied, and when I asked him how he had done so, over his face came a look of pity for this poor stranger, who didn't know how to chop sticks. 'There's an axe in the shed,' he responded, 'I used that. Do you want any more?' 'No thanks James,' I said, but my admiration at the other abilities of a boy who could neither read nor write was unbounded, and I made this very plain to everyone. As he sat at his desk James seemed to grow taller, and he gazed around the room with elation on his face, basking in all this obviously unexpected praise. There was something which he could do at school as well as, or even better than anyone else, and he was proud to have discovered it. From that day on, when James was present, the fire glowed cheerfully, the hearth was swept, and there was a plentiful supply of sticks in the shed and beside the range, all assembled in neat piles. I did not enquire into their origin, which was perhaps just as well, but no-one ever complained!

Jimmy, as I learned to call him, was almost entirely without academic ability, and attended school too rarely to cultivate what little he had; to him, books were a meaningless jumble of black marks, whilst 'James Boyce is late' was all that he could put down on paper unaided. (Later on, I found out that a previous teacher had written that sentence for the class to copy, and eventually, by dint of a supreme effort, Jimmy had also managed to do so, but had been unable to disentangle his name from all the other meaningless symbols.) He tried hard enough and I did my best to help him, but we could accomplish little, so that when he left school at the age of 14, his only other scholastic achievement was the skill needed to use a ruler to draw and measure lines, and so to make simple models, from which he gained a sense of satisfaction second only to his fire-tending activities. He was a popular boy, always happy and good tempered, and seemingly content with that station in life to which God had called him, although it was poor, and greatly lacking in this world's goods. He was big, clumsy and awkward, and not very athletic, yet his greatest times at school were to be in playing a game, which I am sure that he never fully under-stood.

The Kinowla children had little experience of playing any kind of ball game, (partly because of the difficulty of finding any suitable for such a small number of players, so diverse in age, size and strength) but we had devised a game which we called handball. This resembled football, except that the ball was thrown not kicked, and quickly it became very popular. Handball was played with much interest and great enthusiasm, if little skill; it aroused tremendous fervour, which was odd among children who were normally so placid, and choosing teams was most important, for they liked to win! On many occasions when a game was played, Jimmy was absent from school, but at last, his presence coincided with a match. George Regan and Hughie Britton were appointed captains and pro-ceeded to choose the teams; Jimmy was the final choice for he had not played the game before, and his clumsiness was well known, especially to George, who had to take him in his side. George was most disgruntled about this, for his team had lost the last game, and so he wanted more than ever to win this one.

'Jimmy, you play in goal,' George commanded, since players of little worth were always banished to the goal-keeper's posi-tion, a school boy tradition based on the idea that it is the least important position on the field. This order produced nothing but a puzzled look from Jimmy, seeing which, George explained impatiently, 'You stand between those two poles over there and don't let the ball go past you!' With these rudimentary instructions, Jimmy took his place between the tall hazel rods, which served as goalposts, and the game began.

It was soon clear that Hughie's team was the stronger and they began to attack Jimmy's goal. Suddenly the ball was thrown high into the goal-mouth, but Jimmy stuck a big hand up into the air, caught the ball and threw it out again. Another attack developed; this time the ball was slung into the goal at chest height, only for Jimmy to knock it down and clear his line once more. He turned out to have a strong throw and from his long clearance, which landed almost in the opposition's goalmouth, George was able to gather the ball and score, which made him see his goal-keeper in a different light.

Jimmy was the tallest boy in the school, and using his height well, he proved to be impregnable; no throw was too high, or too hard, or too low to elude his grasping hands, whilst his clearances were long and accurate. All the attacks of Hughie's team were frustrated, and from another of Jimmy's immense throws, George's side scored a second time, and won the match by two goals to nil. James Boyce was the hero of the hour, the champion of his team and the envy of their opponents. It was a new experience for him, and much to his liking; the breadth of his smile and the radiance of his face revealed all his joy and exaltation. A new star had been born, and from that day on, whenever handball teams were chosen, and Jimmy was present, he was always the first to be selected, and he did not let his side down, proving to be as difficult to beat as *Cast Iron Bill*, from the pages of *The Rover*. The rarity of his attendance at school however, prevented him from achieving the fullness of his glory, for he never learned to play football, and by the time the boys had begun to play football against other schools, James Boyce had gone out of the school door for the last time.

He found a job with a local farmer, and I did not see him for a long time, until I was leaving Kinowla for another post, some 60 miles away. When all was ready we set off on our journey, but as we approached the main road, a tractor appeared in a field to the right. As was the custom, the driver lifted his hand in greeting, but then, recognising us, he waved it more and more vigorously as he drew nearer. It was James Boyce, and I can still see his wide smile, his hand waving from side to side, and the tractor pursuing an increasingly erratic path, as we paused at the main road until it was clear. We waved back to Jimmy, upon which, leaving the tractor to follow an even more devious path, he waved both his hands until he vanished from our sight; for ever as it proved. A year later, I heard that James had died, killed by a brain tumour, which had finally done its deadly task with merciful speed. Now indeed 'James Boyce is late,' but he is among the first to answer when memory rings the bell.

2 Kinowla Public Elementary School

THE ROAD from the village of Kinowla to the larger village of Derrylummond passed between low, damp fields bordered by hedges, which in springtime were white with hawthorn blossom. It was a minor road, with little traffic, and the children on their way to and from school could meander gently along, and even across, the road without fear of an accident. About a mile from the village was Kinowla Public Elementary School, where at a gap in the hedge, a rough path opened up and led between large areas of grass to the faded blue door of the school, from which the paint was flaking rapidly. In spring and summer the hedges and green grass which surrounded the building were filled with flowers, and the children plaited daisy chains, or picked posies of primroses and violets, which they left upon the teachers' tables in such profusion, that they were often hidden by the heaps of blue, yellow and white.

The only sign that this long, low, once white but now neglected, building was a school, was to be found above the pointed porch where a board inscribed KINOWLA P.E. SCHOOL was displayed. This board was old and weather beaten, the letters were badly formed and uneven, presumably having been made by some anonymous unskilled craftsman, anxious to do what he could for the school and its pupils. No-one knew the age of the board or of the school, but it had stood there for generations with its message of hope through education and enlightenment. From the small porch another door led into the single room of the school, a high gaunt room, but surprisingly light for such an old building, having seven small-paned windows set deep into its thick walls. Sometimes in summer, when the doors were open all day, since it was impossible to open the windows, swallows and other small birds would swoop into the room and fly across it, only to crash headlong into the window which was opposite the door, and fall senseless to the floor. Then there would be a rush of children from their desks, all anxious to cup the tiny quivering body into their warm hands, and carry it outside, where it would quickly recover and fly away once more in the summer sunshine.

Seven long backless desks occupied most of the space in the room, their tops carved with the initials of former scholars, as the school-children, even the most backward, were called locally. I often wondered how all this carving had been done, in view of the strict discipline which, I was told, had existed in the past, for none had been done recently. Certainly it made the desk-tops very uneven, and provided crafty scholars with good excuses for poor writing! Beneath each desk was an open shelf, intended to hold books but useless for that purpose as the floor was so uneven, the desks so unsteady and the shelves so narrow, that the slightest movement sent the books crashing to the floor. The seats were narrow also, and so rough and hard that they must have been most uncomfortable, yet the children never abused the freedom which they were given to warm themselves at the fire, or to 'leave the room' in their own euphemistic phrase, without first seeking permission. Their families had used those desks for so long that any discomfort suffered from unyielding seats had come to be accepted as a fact of school life, for at Kinowla no-one expected to be comfortable at school, and so no-one complained at all. When I had noticed how quiet and well-behaved they were, I had allowed the children to move around at any appropriate moment without first asking me, and it was a trust which was welcomed and respected. A walk, no matter how short, in the fresh air beyond the school door must have come as a moment of much relief to small children, who had wriggled and fidgetted on those merciless benches throughout a long lesson, despite any interest which it might have had for them.

At each end of the room was a blackboard, a cupboard, a table and a chair for each of the two teachers, but there were no other furnishings except for the range at the 'Master's' end. The yellowing walls were rough, and in places huge lumps of plaster seemed destined to fall off at any moment, especially above the fire, where the wall was even more blackened and encrusted with soot than elsewhere. Fortunately none ever did, as if to spite the school inspector's report about the danger of loose plaster, which was just about his only comment upon a building which was quite unfit for the proper education of children. Perhaps if a piece of that plaster had fallen upon a child something might have been done to improve matters, but at least we were spared that, for an injured child would have been far too high a price to pay for any improvement in the school premises. Two or three maps, discoloured with age, hung from the side walls, but for most of the time the disintegrating plaster was decorated with the children's paintings, or posters and other pictures to illustrate work in progress, all of which served to hide the drabness, and enliven the appearance of the sparsely fitted room. Only a few of the children's paintings were really bright for most of them preferred to use darker shades, perhaps because the school building was so ugly and their own homes were so poorly lit.

At that time there was no electricity in the area, so houses were lit by oil-lamps of varying efficiency, and even these were not lit until the last possible moment. Needless to say, we had no lamps of any kind at the school! Apart from the green countryside in which they lived, and the petals of the flowers of the fields and hedgerows, there was little vivid colour in the children's lives, and this was reflected in their art work. Yet, strangely enough, the room was light enough for work to continue until 3. 00 p. m. even on a dark day in winter, without the aid of any artificial light at all, although I recall frequent occasions in better lit schools when electric lights had to be kept on all day. I simply cannot remember or understand how we were able to manage at Kinowla, where only one child wore glasses, despite the lack of illumination.

We had no water either, and each morning two of the biggest boys went to the village to bring back two buckets of water from the pump, a long and tedious chore especially on wet or cold days. At one time a boy had slipped on the icy road when carrying water and had broken his arm, yet still nothing had been done to improve conditions at the school, so perhaps the fall of a chunk of plaster on to a child's head would have had no effect either.

Ironically many modern schools came to resemble this

ancient edifice, for they were built to an open plan, with no
walls dividing the classrooms, but significantly, when at long
last a new school was erected at Kinowla, each classroom was
separate! The old school also had another feature not found in
any of the newest buildings, for against one of the gable walls
was a large covered area with a long bench seat in it, where the
children could play or sit at any time, especially when the
weather was too bad for them to play in the school field. This
was indeed a great boon, as was the field itself, which was
another of the very few advantages which the Kinowla children
enjoyed. It gave them ample space for games of all kinds, whilst
they could also use the two grassy areas at the front, although,
by tradition, these were reserved for quiet occupations like
sewing or working with flowers, chatting to friends or just lying
in the sun. As soon as the weather was warm enough, at
playtime and lunchtime, shoes and socks were swiftly taken off,
and both boys and girls ran barefoot over the grass, rejoicing
in their freedom. One boy, Bobby Harvey, came to school in
bare feet, but only in fine weather, and it was strange to see his
dusty toes projecting beyond the front desk. Although they
liked to play in bare feet, the children always came to school
wearing shoes or boots, and would take care to put them on
again when playtime was over.

Until the 1947 Education Act came into force in April 1948,
all books had to be paid for; even an exercise book cost
fourpence, which is about 10p in current terms, so that few
were used, as the cost was high in terms of the usual family
income. Soon after my arrival at Kinowla, I was visited by the
representative of an educational equipment firm in Belfast,
who sold me a large quantity of exercise books at a reduced
rate, stating that payment would not be required until I had
sold them all to the children. I did not realise just how long this
would take, and when the supply of free books arrived I found
myself with a large number of exercise books for which there
was now no demand at all. However the company was understanding and helpful and took back all the books which were
left. This was just as well, for, as my salary was then £26 per
month, I was in no position to pay for several gross of exercise
books even at a reduced rate! The issue of free books and
materials after 1947 helped immensely in widening the hori-

zons of education in the schoolroom, even though the expenditure allowed was not large, and was the key to many other improvements. There were, of course no school meals, and most children brought their own sandwiches, although a few were able to go home for lunch at mid-day. Free milk was supplied from a large can sent by a local farmer. It was served in thick, heavy, china beakers and was not popular, but later, when the milk came from the creamery, in bottles containing one-third of a pint, and was drunk through a straw, the milk consumption increased dramatically and none was ever left. Many of the children came long distances to school and would have benefitted very much from school meals, more so perhaps, than the town children, who were the first to receive them.

There were two teachers in the school, myself and the infants' teacher, Mrs Hopkins, who had been at Kinowla for all her teaching career. No-one knew just how long that had been, but there were many who would like to have known! She had seen generations of children aged six enter her class, leave her for the 'Master's End' at eight and then pass out into the world at fourteen, or in her earlier days, at an even younger age. Mrs Hopkins bore an awesome responsibility, for the initial literacy of every Protestant child for miles around was in her hands; it was difficult to overcome a poor start and Mrs Hopkins did all she could to ensure that the first steps in reading and writing were taken firmly and with good guidance. Her horizons were limited for she had received no formal training, and had little, if any, educational experience outside of Kinowla, but she had seen a succession of principals come and go, and had remained loyal to her charges, seemingly untroubled by the tremendous burden laid upon her.

These children came from a limited variety of homes but the fathers of most of them were small farmers or farm workers, who worked on wet, ungrateful land to raise a few cattle. The father of one family was a postman, two others kept shops but none of the homes was affluent, and there were few social distinctions between them; all mixed well and there was no pretension or snobbery.

Some of the children lived in the village of Kinowla, which was a tiny hamlet of a few houses, a post office and a shop; it was unusual in Ireland in not having a pub. Thirsts were slaked about four miles away across the border where, at that time, drink was cheaper; strange sights were alleged to have been seen on the way home, on foot or by bicycle, along those four miles of lonely road. One old man claimed to have heard the fairies on the road, after he had dropped some coins from his pocket as he rode his bicycle homeward from the pub one night. Stopping his machine to retrieve the money, he heard the tinkle of tiny voices, which vanished as he drew near to the shillings and half-crowns which shone on the dark road, in the clouded moonlight. To his great disappointment, the fairies, whose voices he had heard, had flown away before he could sight them, but the memory of their silvery speech had remained with him for all the years since he had heard it.

In the village were a Church of Ireland church and a Roman Catholic chapel: the church was perhaps the most striking building in the entire neighbourhood, although it was quite plain, but the stark simplicity of its shape, and the brilliance of its white walls made it stand out among so much that was drab and uninteresting. Certainly the most beautiful man-made object in the district was the stained glass window which filled almost all of the east end of the tiny church; this was a happy combination of modern and traditional design, depicting in vivid colours the theme of the resurrection of Christ. In the background was the hill of Calvary with its three bare crosses; most of the foreground was taken up by the empty tomb of Christ, with the stone rolled away, and surrounded by many brightly coloured flowers, based, I was told, upon the flowers which grew in Palestine during the life of Christ. Linking the two, and dominating the window, was a tremendous shaft of light shining down from Heaven and surrounded by the words, 'He is not here, He is risen', against a sky of pure pale shades, which made an appropriate back-drop for the entire scene. It had been erected by some friends of the church in memory of their son, who had been killed on active service with the army, and it never failed to delight me with its most evocative message and artistry.

The church and the chapel were just across the road from each other, but unfortunately there was no mixing at ecclesiastical level, although community relations of a more general kind were excellent, especially in the wider areas of the countryside. People liked to drop in with neighbours and friends for a chat; this was known as going for a cailey, a word derived from the Irish word 'ceilidhe' meaning an informal dance or get together, and took place without notice or regard of status or religion or anything else, for all doors were open to everyone. On the Twelfth of July some Roman Catholic farmers would milk the cows of their Protestant neighbours to enable them to have a day out, at the celebration of the anniversary of the Battle of the Boyne, whilst on August 15th the roles were reversed as the Roman Catholics kept the Feast of the Assumption, and their Protestant friends looked after their cattle for them.

There was also a Roman Catholic school in the village with about twice as many pupils as Kinowla, but each was isolated from the other, except for one brief contact, when one of the Roman Catholic teachers came to Mrs Hopkins, at the School Inspector's suggestion, for some information about needlework. At this time the village school was going through a difficult period, and some children were leaving it to attend schools in Enniskillen, which was the nearest town, and about 12 miles away. A few of these children walked past Kinowla School each day on their way to catch the early morning bus to the town, and could easily have been enrolled with us, as some parents wished, but this would have been viewed with such disfavour by the church authorities, that they reluctantly sent their children to Catholic schools in the town. It was unfortunate that the trust and friendship which existed socially did not extend to higher levels in the Church.

Some children came to Kinowla on that bus when it made the return journey from Enniskillen, but most walked to school from homes which were scattered over a wide area. Their houses were almost all small and white-washed, with thatched or slated roofs; none had water or electricity so that the children were unused to what was to them luxury, and indeed seemed not to expect it, or even the normal facilities of twentieth century living. Most of the houses were heated by peat fires, which burned on stone hearths at floor level beneath a wide chimney; in some cases these fires were kept in all night by skilful use of ash and fresh turf, and many had not been out for years. Across the fireplace swung a tall iron 'crane' or 'crook', from which were suspended heavy, black metal pots in which food for the family was cooked. Bulbous, three-legged pots, and a flat-bottomed one called the oven, sat around the edge of the fire to be used for baking. And what baking came from those primitive utensils! The dough or cake mixture was put into the oven pot, beneath which glowing peat from the fire was placed, with more burning turf on the lid, and from those pots came superlative bread and cakes, and sponges rising high, delicate and delicious enough, filled as they were with layers of the freshest cream, to tempt even the most weight-conscious of dieters.

Two or three of the houses, where living was less difficult, had coal burning ranges, which were easier to use than the turf fires, but when the range came, the hearth fire was extinguished for the last time, and much atmosphere and tradition were lost. But the housewife, freed from the hard labour of the crook, from the back-breaking tyranny of lifting heavy pots and from stooping low to replenish the fire or to bake, cared little for the lost brightness of the peat-fire flame, and who could blame her?

As they grew older the children were expected to do jobs around the house or farm, feeding the hens, bringing in turf for the fire, or milking the cows, but they had ample space and time to play in the fields, and as they had few toys, they made their own amusement. At night they liked to sit round the fire listening to the talk of their elders, which they seemed to find fascinating, for they sat quietly, never daring to interrupt. They were endowed with, or had acquired, great patience, and were content just to sit in the warmth and glow of the family. That was their good fortune, for almost all of them had homes filled with love, forming a solid foundation to their lives.

They were surrounded by affection, contentment and care, even if that care did not show itself in many material possessions. In many ways they were deprived, with few of the privileges which today's children take for granted, but always they were sure of their family and the continuity of family tradition, which enabled them bravely to face the hardships of everyday living. Their parents and grandparents had lived in much the same manner, and had found happiness in their time: from that experience they had derived the patience, strength and dignity which helped them to find an inner contentment. They had passed those qualities on to their children, who in their turn faced their own problems uncomplainingly, and with the quiet resolution which distinguished all their living.

3 Early Days

'FOR SIX MONTHS of the year Lough Erne is in County Fermanagh, but for the other six months County Fermanagh is in
Lough Erne.' When in November 1947 I saw Kinowla and
County Fermanagh for the first time, I was not aware of this
old saying, but the weather was doing its best to ensure its
truth. Rain, continous rain, thick drenching rain was everywhere, filling the air seemingly without falling, for in Fermanagh
even the rain was gentle, rarely attacking in violent storms,
thrusting down from leaden skies, but persistent, surrounding
and pervading everything with clinging mists. The bare branches
of the trees were fringed with raindrops, which dropped
quickly to the ground, only to be replaced at once by others,
falling inexorably like their predecessors, to extend the pools
which lay everywhere, their surfaces rippled by the descending
droplets and ruffled by the wind. When I think of my first visit
to Fermanagh, I visualise the door of Kinowla School opening
wide to the darkness within, but across its threshold is
the branch of a tree from which raindrops hang like a crystal
pendant. They shimmer but do not fall; they each reflect a tiny
world and shine with a brightness which belies the darkness
of the day. That vision is purely imaginary for no such branch
stretched across the school door, yet the image is vivid and
illustrates much that is true of my experiences in Kinowla. Of
Fermanagh I remember the rain and all my impressions were
gained through a veil of dampness.

The bus from Enniskillen was late of course. At two o'clock
when it should have departed, it was at the stop, but was empty
and there was no sign of the crew, or indeed of any passengers,
but by half-past two, people were drifting into the yard, a driver
and conductor appeared from out of nowhere, and after
another ten minutes wait we were on our way.

After a long journey by train from Belfast I was impatient, and the wet, monotonous countryside which was vaguely visible through the steamy windows, did little to allay my frustration at the long delay. However I was soon to learn that this lack of worry about time was indicative of an attitude that time was made for man and not vice-versa; as John Britton was to say to me on many later occasions, 'The man who made time made plenty of it.'

My destination was Skenbarra, a small town in what is now the Irish Republic, and my somewhat melancholy feelings vanished at once when I was met there by the Reverend Brian Davey, whose parish included Skenbarra and Kinowla, and who was the sole manager of Kinowla Public Elementary School. He was bright and cheerful, and the warmth of his welcome and that of his wife Margaret, soon made me forget the rain and the uncomfortable journey which I had had. They were to become our firm friends, but their friendship was never more welcome than during those first few hours of our meeting.

Next day I walked into the school for the first time and thought that it was a bare and unattractive place, but somehow it did not seem to be inhospitable, despite the cold, the dampness and its air of neglect. Is any schoolroom attractive when it is without children, and lifeless?

However it was with mixed feelings that I then went with Brian Davey to the farmhouse, where John Britton lived with his family. John was a quiet man, whose bright blue eyes contrasted with his weather-beaten wrinkled skin, and as we talked, his wife, whom we were always to know as Mrs Britton, busied herself making the first of many cups of tea which I was to have beside the big hearth fire in the farm kitchen. Never before had I tasted tea like it; permeated with the peaty tang of the water from which it had been made, and tinged with the peat smoke from the fire, its taste was unique in my experience, but it was offered with a kindliness that overcame any scruples about taste. We sat on the long wooden settle near the fire, and at the back of the room, quiet, but attentive to all that was going on, were the children, their eyes upon this stranger, who might become their new master.

John had a house named Carrick Cottage, which he was
prepared to let to the incoming teacher, so we went to see it;
a long, low whitewashed cottage with a brown door and window
frames, and a roof of yellow thatch. For many people, to live in
the country in a thatched cottage would be the realisation of a
dream, but Carrick Cottage was not at all dreamlike, even
though the rain had ceased and a wintry sun was doing its best
to add some sparkle to the scene. To my town-bred eyes it was
decidedly spartan but there were fields at the back, leading to
a tree-clad hill, and the rushing of water sounded merrily from
a stream running alongside the hill path, just behind the tall
trees in the corner of the large garden. Already I had learned
not to expect electricity but I was pleased when John said,
'There's a good supply of water here, so you needn't worry
about that.' 'Good,' I said looking round, 'but where are the
taps?' 'Taps!' he exclaimed. 'There aren't any taps!' 'Where do
we get the water from, then?' I asked. 'If it's rough water for
washing,' John replied, 'you can get it from the stream across
the road,' – the sound of the stream was now much less musical
to me – 'but the drinking water comes from a spring-well at the
back. Come with me and I'll show you.'

He was wearing wellingtons and so the walk across two fields,
saturated by the recent rains, affected him little, but it soaked
my city shoes, and the legs of my trousers became first damp,
then wet, and then soggy. John grew excited when we reached
the well, which was hidden by long grass. Bending down, he
pulled the grass aside and said, 'There's the drinking water.
Look how fresh and clean it is!' and cupping his hands, he
lifted some water and drank it, with the relish of a wine
connoisseur approving some fine new vintage. Then, taking
a short step sideways, he parted another tuft of long wet
grass and said with a note of pride in his voice, 'Now look at
this. Where else could you find two such wells so close together?' They both looked the same to me, just pools of water
surrounded by stones, with lank grass hanging heavily over
them; what was so remarkable about that?

Excitedly John went on, 'Go on, take a drink, it'll do you
good,' and he drank again, with even more delight than
before. 'It's only water,' I thought, 'why's he so excited?,' but
obediently I bent down, scooped up some water in my hands

and drank it. I soon wished that I had not, and spluttered in distaste, for the water was somehow warmish and had a sulphur-like taste, which I did not like at all. 'Ugh!,' I exploded, 'What on earth is that?' John thought this very funny and laughed. 'Did you not like it? It's spa water and is good for rheumatism,' he said and proceeded to take several large draughts of the sulphur water to show me just how good it was. Apparently it was uncommon to find two such different wells so close together, but the importance of this fact receded before my need to get rid of the taste of this awful water, which I never drank again. At least my taste buds were being stimulated this eventful morning, for peaty tea and spa water were two new gastronomical experiences for them, but they did not care much for either.

Margaret Davey's lunch proved to be more acceptable, and it was with a sense of well-being that I said goodbye to Brian, promising to let him know if I would accept the post, after I had discussed it with my wife. Throughout the several hours of the journey back to Belfast, I wondered what to do. Undoubtedly life at Kinowla would not be easy, the school was in poor condition and badly equipped, the house was not at all what I had hoped it would be and I knew that it would mean much hard work for Elizabeth, without any modern appliances to help her. If I took the job, it would mean living among strangers in an environment foreign to any that we had known; yet the hospitality I had been shown, and the warmth of the welcome given to me, glowed around my mind. I recalled also the children whom I had met, their shy but pleasant manner and their quiet yet lively eyes; I thought that I should like them and that we could work well together.

Elizabeth met me at the station and we talked about the situation long into the night. Kinowla School might not be modern but at least the children promised to be rewarding to teach; Carrick Cottage was no mansion but it would be our first home together and this would mean much to us both; nothing was ideal but it was a start, and we thought that we could settle down there, despite all the apparent difficulties. Next morning I wrote to Brian Davey to tell him that I would accept the post of Principal Teacher of Kinowla Public Elementary School from the beginning of the next term, Monday 5th January, 1948...

Brian Davey said, 'You must come to the Christmas party. It will give you a chance to meet Mrs Hopkins and some of the children, and anyway I'm sure that you'll enjoy it.' The Christmas party was held on New Year's Day, and was a muted but happy occasion, especially for children unaccustomed to party games as I knew them. It was a look back into the past, with a very old-fashioned   atmosphere; the children played 'The Farmer Wants a Wife,' 'Take Her Off to Wembley', and similar games, all of which were dated, even in my childhood. Music was provided by a solo fiddler who, like his fellow-musician in Thomas Hardy's *Under the Greenwood Tree*, became so engrossed in his music, that he 'sawed madly at the strings, with legs firmly spread and eyes closed, regardless of the visible world.' The white cloth, which he had placed across his shoulder to protect his jacket from wear, had slipped to his lap, but he ignored this, and still played on frantically, with the chair upon which he sat, moving farther and farther back, until it seemed inevitable that, sooner or later, it would collide with the rear wall of the stage. Fortunately however, the games and dancing were interrupted by the serving of refreshments, and the fiddler opened his eyes, stuffed the cloth into his pocket, brought the chair forward to its starting place and, freed from the quivering intensity of his music making, re-entered the world of ordinary mortals.

Earlier on I had been introduced to Mrs Hopkins, a tall lady with a gushing manner, who welcomed me effusively. 'I'm sure that you will like it here,' she enthused. 'You must meet some of my friends. We'll go to Fernagh and meet Lord and Lady Morrell; you'd like that, wouldn't you?' It hadn't taken her long to bring her acquaintance with the local aristocracy into the conversation, and it never did, for it was a source of much pride to her, and of mild amusement to all who knew her. However it was a harmless foible, and neither added nor detracted from her standing locally, although she loved to speak of her titled friends to anyone who would listen.

During the interlude in the party, Mrs Hopkins came to me. 'Mr Claypole,' she asked, 'I wonder if you would please make the presentation to Mr Hanna for us? As you are coming to take his place, that would be nice wouldn't it?' Mr Hanna was the untrained teacher, who had been teaching at Kinowla for about a year, and was now going to teacher training college, so I agreed readily. Immediately Mrs Hopkins clapped her hands, and called out, 'Quiet please! Mr Claypole has kindly agreed to make the presentation to Mr Hanna,' then thrust a small parcel into my hands and sat down. I was nonplussed and at a loss to understand the reason for this great haste, especially as I had met Mr Hanna only a little while before and knew very little about him. Nevertheless I made a conventional speech of thanks and good wishes, and handed over the present, still bewildered by the speed of it all - it was the first time I had known anything to happen quickly at Kinowla, and I was to learn that such speed was very rare!

When the party resumed Brian Davey spoke to me. 'You fell for that all right,' he said. 'Why did you do it?' Realising that he meant the presentation, I answered, 'Well, I could hardly refuse, when Mrs Hopkins asked me, could I? What's wrong with it anyway?' This was my introduction to the maze of little intrigues which can bedevil (or enliven!) country life. It seemed that there had been agreement about giving the present, but disagreement about its organisation, so that no-one suitable locally had been prepared to hand it over. Hence when Mrs Hopkins had conceived the idea of asking me to do it, and when I had agreed, she had hurried on with the ceremony before I could be warned about what was happening. Brian was displeased at this, because he thought that I had been deceived, but I found it amusing, and after all was I not becoming acquainted with Mrs Hopkins and her ways, just as he had said I should?

Next morning, I entered Kinowla School for the first time as its Principal Teacher. The Christmas holidays had not yet ended and the school was cold and empty, its walls bare of any kind of decoration. The grubby maps which hung here and there could not be termed decorative as they were tarnished and faded with age; on another wall was a small blackboard, apparently used to record the attendance of each class daily, and next to it hung an imposing, but yellowing document headed 'TIMETABLE.' This document had been completed a long time ago, the ink in which it was written had faded, and a smear of dust covered the front. When I turned the timetable over, I noticed that the card on which it was mounted, was the

base of a large cobweb. Symbolically perhaps, I brushed away
the dust and removed the cobweb, before studying the list of
subjects to be taught; it consisted mainly of English, Arithmetic
and Handwriting, with occasional attention given to Singing,
Needlework and Physical Training. Algebra and Geometry
were also included but no Geography, History, Nature Study or
Art. I was fresh from college where I had been greatly impressed
by R. L. Russell's remarks in his book *The child and his pencil*, about
the need for breadth and imagination in the curriculum of
rural elementary schools, so I took out my pen and with a bold
flourish, drew a thick, black line through algebra and geometry, which I decided, had no relevance to the needs of the
children at Kinowla, even those aged eleven and over. Most if
not all of them, I reasoned, would work on farms when they left
school and they would not require algebra and geometry
there; better by far to teach them something about the world,
to widen their horizons and to stimulate their imaginations
with great literature and poetry, than to cramp them with
quadratic equations and congruent triangles. It was the arro-
gance of inexperience of course, yet I still feel that in the
circumstances it was a good change. In any case I found that
algebra and geometry had not been taught at Kinowla for
many years; originally they had been entered on the timetable
when teachers had been paid extra for teaching them, and had
lapsed into dis-use when such payments had ceased. I must
stress that my own dislike of mathematics played no part at all
in the decision!

I took the roll-book home with me, and that evening studied
the names of the children in the various classes, reading for
the first time names which were to become so familiar to me,
and which still wander widely through my mind, and all with
affection, even after so many years. Mark Britton, Charles
Taylor, Peter and Elizabeth Carr, and all the others, children then but grown up now, many with children of their own;
their faces are still fresh in my memory, although others, first
seen much more recently in different places, have faded
completely. Yet I was so raw that I was surprised when I realised
how few were in each class: how could I possibly organise
them?

There was to be no cause for alarm, for they organised

themselves. On the first morning after the holidays, the scholars came into the room quietly, a little apprehensive about the
new Master, though probably less so than I was about them.
They sat in their accustomed places, and waited for me to
reveal myself, although they knew what was going to happen,
for they had been prepared for it by their own experience, and
by long years of family tradition. Even the two children who
were at school that day for the first time, seemed to be at home.
They had been brought to school by older brothers or sisters,
who had taken off their coats for them, before leaving the
newcomers with Mrs Hopkins and then going to their own
seats. No parents had appeared, and no special arrangements
had been made, but the children's life at school had commenced
calmly and happily, with no fuss at all.

It is different today, and rightly so, for it is still important that
children should settle down happily at school as quickly as
possible. In modern conditions, with bigger schools, this is
more difficult than it was in places like Kinowla, with their
smaller numbers and family atmosphere; it is essential to
involve parents, and to ease children into school gently, by
staggering entries, or by allowing them to come for a short
time, before entering upon the rigours of a full school day. I
taught in two rural schools for 11 years, and this was not
necessary in either of them, but it certainly was in the town
schools, in the later stages of my career. There is a popular
rhyme *Wee Hughie*, well known to generations of Ulster folk,
which begins:

'He's gone to school, wee Hughie, and him not four
Sure I saw the fright was on him, when he left the
door.'

and ends:

'I followed to the turnin, and when they passed it by,
God help him he was cryin, and maybe so was I. '

but there is no mention of the mother accompanying Hughie,
and despite his tears and her obvious worries about him, the
idea of taking him to school for his first day has never crossed
her mind. The poem says, 'He took a hand o' Benny, and a
hand o' Dan' for that was the natural thing to do. They would
look after Hughie and that would be enough. I am pleased to
say that I do not recall any first day tears at Kinowla.

I am reminded of an incident which happened to me many years later in England, when a mother brought a small girl aged four to school to enrol her for admission. As usual I spoke to the child and asked her to tell me her name. She lowered her head and said, 'Shan't tell.' I was surprised and replied, 'Oh! Come on you can tell me. I know the names of all the girls and boys in our school. Will you tell me your name, please?' With a little pout of the lips she said again, 'Shan't tell.' I turned to the mother and asked her the name of her daughter, who obviously was not going to tell me herself. 'But she's already told you,' she answered. 'Her name's Chantelle.' and to make it doubly clear, she spelt it for me; CHANTELLE. There were no Chantelles at Kinowla, where the children's names were plain and familiar ones like Elizabeth and Margaret, and David and George, so that later in the day, I was able to deal easily with the enrolment of the new entrants, although we were all new and strange.

With an outward show of confidence hiding a feeling of great nervousness, I called the roll and then divided my class into two groups, gave the younger ones some work to do, and devoted my attention to the older children in the back desks. They were expecting this, so out came the arithmetic books, the pens and the pencils, and they were most surprised when I asked them to put everything anyway, and we started to discuss various topics which I thought might interest them. Never has there been a more one-sided discussion for it was almost impossible to persuade them to say anything beyond 'Yes' and 'No.' They were not being obstinate or unhelpful, but were shy and unaccustomed to speaking to strangers, even those with the best of intentions and the highest of motives.

Quickly tiring of this, I asked the children to take out a book which they were reading, and all of them produced a volume with red covers, which was about a traveller in Northern Canada in the mid-nineteenth century. I have never seen such an unattractive book. Its name, which mercifully I have forgotten, was printed in black type upon the dark red covers, and could hardly be distinguished. The pages were covered with print so small and so closely packed, that, inside the margins the paper appeared to be almost black, and a search for a picture was in vain. It was a long book too; nearly 300 pages of tiny black type - enough to frighten anyone from reading for life.

One by one the children read aloud to me, one or two with fluency, some with mistakes and long pauses, but none with interest or real understanding. We carried on until all had read at least a line or two, but it was hard going for them to master the words and for me to endure having to hear so much effort being wasted on such poor material. Even I was relieved, when with a sigh I admitted defeat and said, 'Very well. Please take out your arithmetic books and show me what you've been doing.'

Each day we continued to struggle through the pages of this colourless book, and our progress was almost as slow as that of the intrepid traveller whose story it told, making his way by sledge across the icy Arctic wastes. 'Surely,' I thought, 'there must be something I can do to make reading more interesting than this.' What was available for them to read, which was more relevant to them than these outdated memoirs? Then one evening the answer came to me in a lightning flash of inspiration and the single word 'Newspapers!' Of course, of course, the children could all bring the previous day's paper to school, and we could read the news together. I could hardly wait to go to school the next day to see their reaction. When we opened the dreaded red covers, I said to the class, 'What do you think of this book?,' and expected eventually to hear complaints of dullness and boredom for I thought that the awfulness of the book might help to loosen their tongues a little. Instead I received just blank stares from everyone, and it took me some time to convince them that I really wanted their opinions about the book. They seemed genuinely surprised to be asked; it was as if no-one had ever sought their ideas before, and certainly not about the book which they were reading with such tortoise-like slowness. After all they had had no choice in the matter; the book had no doubt been chosen because it was cheap and readily available, then thrust into their hands to be worked through to the end, whether they liked it or not. Reading the book was to them just another job to be done and they would continue with it until it was finished, just as a farmer would plough a field until the task was completed. At last however, after some prompting, the replies came, many of them halting and poorly expressed but genuine and sincere.

'It's not interesting. I don't like it.'

'The words are too hard for me.'

'There aren't any pictures.'

'It's a good book and tells you about the man's hard times in the ice and snow.'

At least one liked the book very much, but the general boredom was evident, and at last I produced my wonderful idea. With great pride, as if announcing some unique event I said, 'You don't like the book do you? Very well from tomorrow we'll be reading something different and much more interesting. I'd like you to bring a newspaper to school and we'll read the paper instead of the book.'

This was met with even less enthusiasm than the daily opening of the awful book, and I was astonished, for I had felt sure that this masterpiece of creative thinking on my part, would have had the children bubbling in their seats with excitement. Instead they looked at one another and then gazed back at me, with their usual impassive stares. This should have warned me, but instead I said weakly, 'Please bring a newspaper to school tomorrow and we'll read that.' Once they start, I thought, they will become as excited as I am, but for the moment however, the huskies were harnessed to the sledges, which hissed their way across the ice, to the accompaniment of stammers and stumbles and the restless shifting of impatient feet, many of them clad in hob-nailed boots, which made almost as much noise as the barking dogs, the shouting men and the running sledges depicted in the book.

Next day I took reading with the senior group as the very first lesson, so keen was I to proceed with my wonderful idea.

'Have you brought the newspapers?', I asked, and seeing one or two heads nod, I went on, 'Good, please take them out, and we'll read them now.' I waited with eager expectation for the rustle of at least a dozen papers being taken out, for although there were 18 children in the group, even I had not thought that they would all bring one. Instead, four newspapers appeared; two copies of the *Irish Daily Telegraph*, each for a different day, an old copy of the *Daily Express*, and an edition of the local paper, the *Impartial Reporter* which was two weeks old. The failure of my scheme surprised and upset me, I had not expected 18 papers, but four copies, and all of them different, was not very encouraging.

'What's wrong?,' I remonstrated with them. 'Did you forget to bring a paper with you? Surely this isn't the best you can do?' Unfortunately for me it was, for I was to discover that very few of the families took a newspaper at all, apart from the local paper, the *Impartial Reporter*, which was published weekly, and read so fully and avidly, that the children could not be allowed to bring it to school, lest they did not take it home again; after all mum and dad might not have finished reading every single word of it, including all the small advertisements for Rhode Island Red pullets at 'point of lay!' In face of this I was compelled, or so I thought, to abandon my great idea, and continue our travels across Canada. I was too inexperienced to know that in teaching, very little happens quickly, especially in rural places like Kinowla, and so it is important to persevere, even when plans seem to be impossible to carry out. Now I realise that I could have asked the class to bring old copies of the *Impartial Reporter*, for at least some would have been the same, and we could have managed with them. However, I gave in too easily and we were condemned to spending more weary days traversing the Canadian Arctic, when we might have been enthralled by reading of the activities of the local churches, or the Fermanagh County Council, or even of the cases at the courts around the county. Perhaps northern Canada might have been more interesting after all!

Nevertheless the episode brought to my attention the *Irish Daily Telegraph*, a newspaper of which, until then, I had never heard. It was a morning version of the previous evening's *Belfast Telegraph*, and circulated in the more remote parts of the province, to which, presumably the evening paper could not be delivered on the day of publication. I was also given cause to think about the *Impartial Reporter*. Was there ever a more splendid name for a newspaper, and its full title was even more resplendent: *The Impartial Reporter and Farmers' Journal for Fermanagh, Cavan, Leitrim, North Monaghan and South Tyrone, incorporating The Erne Packet 1808.* Although the paper was first published in 1825 its name has a grand 18th century sonority about it, and its readers should surely be dressed in wigs and knee breeches, instead of the tweed trousers and caps

(worn with the peaks to the back as was the Fermanagh style)
of its masculine readers in 1948.

All that seems a long time ago, yet even as late as 1958 I did
not receive the *Manchester Guardian*, in an easily accessible
village, 12 miles from Londonderry, until 7. 30. p. m. , and even
then only by the courtesy of three intermediaries. . . . four on
Young Farmers' Club nights! There have been many changes
in the delivery of newspapers to Northern Ireland since then!

Other things have changed also, and the changes occasioned
by the 1947 Northern Ireland Education Act were all to the
good; no longer was the cost of books and equipment the only
factor in their choice, and I am certain that no teacher would
have chosen the Canadian book, except for its cheapness. I was
fortunate of course, for the benefits of the Act began to be felt
when I had been teaching for only three months, and they were
indeed many. The initial allocation to Kinowla was only £32,
yet it was worth far more than that for the freedom of choice
which it gave. It did not extend as far as Mrs Hopkins' requisition for needlework materials, which was for about £60,
although I had told her about the total for the requirements of
the entire school. Even after my requests and long explanations,
she could not reduce it to less than £30, so that I was compelled
to allocate to her an amount of only a few pounds, with which
she was well content, and which was of course, much more
than she had ever spent before on needlework materials.

In those early days of the scheme, it was difficult to persuade
the administrators to give the teachers full freedom in pur-
chasing items for use in their schools, and we were allowed to
choose from a very limited list of materials, which was known
as the Schedule, although there was no restriction on the
choice of books. For some time I fought a losing battle against
this; my requests for unscheduled items causing some consternation in the office of the County Fermanagh Education
Committee, where, it seemed, no-one had ever thought about
consulting teachers about what should be made available. I
suspect, however, that this was not due to any obstinacy on their
part, but rather because, in administering a completely new
scheme, they were reluctant to add to their burden of work,
and were insufficiently acquainted with the needs of their
schools. This was confirmed some years later, after I had

submitted a list of items which might be added to the Schedule of the County Tyrone Education Committee, only to be told that 'the educational contractors were pressing for the Schedule to be reduced not increased.' This made me angry, as it seemed to be a gross misunderstanding of the administration of the free books and materials scheme, and I replied, asking who should choose equipment for schools, the suppliers or the teachers? I received no reply, a favourite gambit of educational adminstrators everywhere when faced with awkward questions, but all the things for which I had asked were on the approved Schedule for the following year, so I suppose I should have been grateful!

I devote much attention to all this, because I think that the provision of free books and materials was a vital educational advance in Northern Ireland, and opened the door to many areas of development and growth. New methods of teaching almost always require new materials and extra equipment, and their provision would have been impossible if children had still been responsible for supplying their own educational needs.

The 1947 Education Act also made other changes in the provision of educational opportunities, and most important of these for the children of Kinowla was the introduction of the 11+ examination, then known in Northern Ireland as the 'Qualifying.' Children aged 10 could take this examination and if they passed it, could attend a grammar school without payment. Undoubtedly this was a tremendous advance for the many children of the necessary academic ability, whose parents could not possibly afford to pay grammar school fees, or indeed to provide the necessary uniform, books etc. , to say nothing of transport costs, which were high, especially in country areas like Kinowla, where the nearest grammar school was 12 miles away. It is my belief now, that on balance, the 11+ examination was not a good educational development, for it led to many doubtful practices, among them the tendency to concentrate upon academic children, and the consequent narrowing of the curriculum for all, since the worth of a school in the eyes of many people, was judged by the number of its pupils who passed the Qualifying. Of course this was wrong, as was the feeling of failure among those who did not pass; such feelings were unnecessary, but they did occur because of the

attitudes of the public, and they were much to the detriment
of many children and their schools. These attitudes still exist
today, despite the growth of an excellent system of secondary
education for all, and still they do harm to true educational
values.

Before 1948 however, no such system existed, so that children at Kinowla Public Elementary School whose parents
could not afford to pay grammar school fees, remained there
until they reached the age of 14 and then left school. As none
of the families was so affluent, all the children stayed on at the
Elementary School, and so could receive only the very limited
education given there, studying a narrow range of subjects,
and probably being taught by only two teachers during the
whole of their time at school. I was acutely aware of this, and
even at the end of my career as a teacher, had to fight off the
idea that I must tell the children about Beethoven or Shakespeare, for if I didn't, then no-one else would, as once they left
my class, they had finished with school for ever.

With the advent of the Qualifying Examination, all this
changed for at least a few of our children each year, as passing
the exam. enabled them to attend a larger school, to meet a
wider range of pupils and teachers, to study new fields of
knowledge and to find new interests to explore. The majority
continued at Kinowla, and not until the building of new
Secondary Intermediate Schools in the 1950s and 1960s, were
the benefits of change and expansion given to all. In the
meantime the doors of Portora Royal School, (the school of
Oscar Wilde, Samuel Beckett and H. F. Lyte, the author of *Abide
With Me*), and of Enniskillen Collegiate School were opened to
boys and girls, whose educational lives had hitherto been
confined to schools like Kinowla. It was an opportunity which
they grasped eagerly. In 1967, a new school was opened at
Kinowla, and its first headmaster was Colin Taylor, who, in
1948, had been the first child at the old school to pass the
Qualifying Examination.

4   *Widening Horizons*

'THIS IS **BBC** Radio for Schools,' announced the impeccably English voice from the tiny loudspeaker. 'Stories from History.' The children sat still and expectant, even Mrs Hopkins' class at the other end of the room, much preferred this strange voice to the well-known one of their teacher, who, in any case, was listening to it herself. This was new to everyone, for none of them had seen a radio set in school before and all were curious to hear what was going to happen. It happened very suddenly. The radio voice went on. 'Episode Five – The Spanish Armada,' and then the air was filled with a vast gale, howling and whistling through the rigging of a sailing ship, almost drowning the hoarse cries of Spanish officers, screaming orders into the wind. But the broadcast itself was drowned in a new gale, a gale of laughter from almost all the children, which continued for what seemed an age until they became accustomed to the sounds from the loudspeaker, and settled down to listen, in their usual quiet manner, to the interplay of voices which followed the highly dramatic introduction to the story.

Once more I was in the state of bewilderment, which had been my constant companion since coming to Kinowla School, for bringing the radio to school had seemed a good idea to me, as I was sure that it would interest the children and bring new voices and fresh ideas into the classroom. I had not anticipated laughter, certainly not at the Spanish Armada, and was at a loss to understand what had happened to amuse them so much. It had never occurred to me that some of the children might never have heard a radio before; after all this was 1948, radio was commonplace and had played a significant part in conveying news of the World War, which had ended only two and a half years earlier, surely, even to remote places like Kinowla. Some

33

parts of the country were on the threshold of the television age by this time. Yet this was indeed the case. For many children in the class, this was the very first time they had heard a radio. Some of the others had heard news broadcasts, but only a few had ever listened to imaginative programmes such as the one which had caused so much apparent hilarity.

However, I was unaware of this until, some time later, I read a social study of rural life in Northern Ireland, which contained a survey of a nearby area, where some of the children lived. The statistical tables showed that 38% of the houses surveyed had a radio set, but there was a footnote, stating that the researchers had discovered that many of the sets did not work, so that they thought it more accurate to estimate that only 19% of homes had a radio, which could receive programmes! There is no doubt that this would apply to the entire Kinowla district, and so it was not surprising that the tempestuous wind and the shouting sailors should have caused so much consternation, and indeed, apprehension. But why the laughter?

Some years later a school inspector enabled me to answer that question. I was then teaching in another school and, for the inspector's benefit, the class had just sung a lullaby by Mozart, which they had learned from a radio programme. Their performance had been a good one, in tune and with a sweet round tone, and I was very pleased with them. Mr James, the inspector, was pleased also and said, 'Well done! That was lovely. Now I'll sing it to you in Mozart's own language.' Perching himself on a corner of my table, he began to sing in a clear firm voice, 'Schlafe, mein Prinzlein, schlafe,' and continued in German to the end of the verse, but was then unable to carry on, for at the first pause, the children, unable to contain themselves any longer, had burst out into loud laughter, just as the class at Kinowla had done, upon hearing the gale on the radio. Fearing the effect of this display upon Mr James's report on the school, I was upset and embarrassed, but he was completely calm and understanding.

'Don't worry,' he said, 'that's only to be expected. When anything strange or unusual happens to us, we either want to laugh or cry. It was really my fault, for I should have warned them that it would sound different from their singing. I'm glad that they chose to laugh and not to cry!' When the laughter had subsided, he went on to sing the remaining verses, and at the end he was greeted with a round of applause. . . the report was safe after all!

The sounds of the Spanish Armada, Mozart sung in German, the reception of both had been the same, and the laughter had been caused by surprise not amusement, but I was glad that the children had not been frightened by what they had heard, if only because I did not think that I could have coped with the resulting tears!

In such an isolated school as Kinowla, the Schools' Radio broadcasts were of immense value in bringing different ideas and personalities into the classroom. By means of that tiny blue box, we could hear stories and songs, music and plays; we could travel to India or Africa, meet people who lived in Australia or Russia, cross the Atlantic with Columbus or learn how tulips are grown in Holland; the radio was a window on the world, and important in widening limited horizons and stretching imaginations, which could so easily remain dormant and dull. Yet in March 1949, a prominent member of the County Tyrone Education Committee was reported as saying, 'If schools are provided with wireless sets, the children will know the results of all the big races'! At the end of that year, the County Fermanagh Education Committee, ever vigilant and cautious, postponed for one year, making any decision about the supply of radio sets to their schools. They need not have worried about Kinowla School, for the radio in use was the one from home, where it was a precious link with the world outside; a request to the Ministry of Education for a grant towards the cost of expensive, and heavy, batteries to be kept in the school, brought a letter, one sentence long, of about 10 lines and at least 100 words, saying, 'No!'

Although it took place 42 years ago, there is one broadcast which I recall with great clarity because of the almost hypnotic effect which it had upon the children who listened to it, and that meant the entire school for it quickly had even Mrs Hopkins and her 'wee ones' under its spell. It was by J. Morpurgo, and dealt with the development of railways in the U. S. A. and the growth of Chicago as a city and as a railway centre. Beginning with the story of Kitty McShane's cow, which is alleged to have kicked over a lamp in its byre, and so to have

started the Great Fire of Chicago in 1871, it went on to describe
the spread of the railroad and the rise of the city with its
stations, skyscrapers and stockyards. I remember vividly a
simple folk-song which, with a rhythmic guitar accompaniment, ran through the broadcast. I had never heard it before,
and have not heard it since, but still it haunts my memory. The
song began,

> 'I wouldn't marry a farmer
> He's always in the dirt,
> I'd rather marry an engineer'.

and threaded its way through the story. Although the events
described had taken place long ago and so far away, and were
utterly remote from their experience, for most of them had
never even seen a train, the children listened spellbound, and
an electric atmosphere built up, which was slow to subside,
even when the switch clicked to end the programme, and
returned us all to reality.

   This was my first true experience in school of the grip of the
imagination, the spell of the Ancient Mariner's tale; it was to
happen again later, on treasured occasions, which I recall even
now with pleasure and excitement. Two examples come instantly to mind; the first early one Monday morning, when 300
childen sitting on a hard wooden floor, listened with intense,
enthralled attention to a record of the slow movement of the
Mendelssohn Violin Concerto, and the remembered music
remained, hovering in the air around us, long after the real
notes had passed into silence. Music did not always have that
effect, but it was achieved unfailingly whenever I read to the
children, either in class or at assembly, 'The Selfish Giant' by
Oscar Wilde. No matter what the circumstances were, or how
often they had heard it before, when I read that tender story
and finished its final sentence, 'And when the children ran in
that afternoon, they found the Giant lying dead under the tree,
all covered with white blossoms.' the reaction was always the
same, a hushed silence and an air of great poignancy, so
delicate that even one everyday word seemed to shatter it. The
story worked its magic on all the children from the wide-eyed
four-year-olds to the would-be tough guys of the top Junior
class; all seemed to respond to the simplicity of its language and
the beauty of its ideas, including the School Meals staff, who

would open their kitchen serving hatch into the Assembly Hall, in order to listen to the story themselves.

Taking even a small radio set to school wasn't always easy, for it could be difficult for me to ride a bicycle, whilst carrying the allegedly portable set in my right hand, with a bag of books suspended from the other side of the handlebars. Fortunately there was little traffic, but one day, when I was also carrying a large parcel, I was accosted by a new and vigilant policeman from the local station, who was known as 'Bells and Brakes,' because of his insistence on checking all bicycles which were brought to his attention, and prosecuting the unlucky owner if defects were found. Constable McMillan was reputed to hide in a nearby hedge late at night, when local dances were being held, in order to spring out upon cyclists who were riding homewards without lights, or appeared to be unsteady upon their machines. I do not know if this actually happened, but certainly one day when I called to see John Britton, who was a Justice of the Peace, I found him signing 47 summonses, all of them issued by 'Bells and Brakes!'

When he saw me coming, Constable McMillan alighted from his own bicycle, and signalled to me to stop, which in view of my many burdens, I could do only with some difficulty. 'Where are you going?, he demanded, after I had wobbled to a precarious halt, and was trying to stop the parcel from falling on to the wet road. 'I'm going to the school,' I replied, staring pointedly at the bag of blue covered exercise books, the address label on the parcel and the radio set, which was suspended from my right hand. 'Oh yes,' he retorted, with disbelief in his voice. 'Who are you?' To be fair he had never set eyes on me before, but it seemed obvious who I was. Who else but a teacher would be approaching a school with a pile of exercise books? 'I'm the Master. My name's Mr Claypole.' His face did not change for some while, and I was beginning to envisage the report in the *Impartial Reporter* - 'LOCAL TEACHER IN COURT. RIDING BICYCLE DANGEROUSLY. CONSTABLE'S VIGILANCE PRAISED,' and was wondering how much the fine would be, for even the smallest amount would be too big to pay from my meagre salary. But such fame was to be denied to me, for at last the hard face creased into a smile, and the policeman said, 'I'm sorry Mr Claypole, I didn't recognise you. Let me carry that parcel for you.'

With that, this keen guardian of the law took the parcel, placed it across the handlebars of his official mount, and rode off to the school, leaving me to follow steadily in his wake, both of us riding our machines in an unlawful manner, but with no hint of a summons, even from the dreaded 'Bells and Brakes' - and my bike did not have a bell anyway!

When we reached the school the constable carried the parcel to my table, and returned for the radio set, which he took in to the classroom also. Assuring me of his help at all times, he waved a cheery 'Goodbye' to the astonished children and myself, and cycled off to resume his duties. Even 'Bells and Brakes' was human!

Shortly afterwards Constable McMillan was transferred to a small town in another part of Fermanagh, where he achieved notoriety by taking to court, the son of the local inspector of police, for some minor fault with his bicycle. He was moved again, very quickly, and for some reason, never stayed for long at any station!

Normally I took the radio to school myself, but sometimes, if Elizabeth wanted to listen to a programme I would leave the set at home and she would bring it to me later. Our house was about a mile from the school, and all sorts of people would be pressed into service to carry the set, from the rare passing motorist, to farmers with a horse and cart, on their way to the creamery, or the shop in the village. Often she would bring it herself on her own bike, and on one occasion she was unfortunate enough to fall from the machine into the hedge, where the radio fell from her hand. She called at the Britton's house, where Mrs Britton attended to her cuts and bruises and gave her a cup of tea, before allowing her to proceed to the school.

When Elizabeth arrived, it was almost time for the broadcast to begin, and I was anxious and annoyed that she should be so late. Without seeking any explanation for the delay, I grabbed the radio, hastened into the school and switched the set on. Nothing happened so I switched it off and on again several times, but still it remained obstinately silent. Having been a radar mechanic with the R.A.F., I applied the time-honoured method of repairing recalcitrant radios, and gave the set a hefty thump, but stubborn as ever, it still refused to function, and even further violent attacks failed to make it change its mind. That day we had no radio programme, and only when I returned home did I discover what had happened to Elizabeth and the radio. No wonder it didn't work! It took some time for the set to be repaired, and it cost me £7, which was more than a week's salary! But I thought that it was in a good cause, since I was convinced that listening to schools' broadcasts was valuable experience to the Kinowla children, and helped greatly in widening their interests and stimulating their minds. Of course, the radio was essential to Elizabeth and myself if we were to keep up with events in the outside world, far from Kinowla, and sometimes, seemingly, on another planet.

Some time after my encounter with 'Bells and Brakes,' the police called at the school to ask if they might show some road safety films to the children and of course I agreed, although I was unable to understand why, as cars were rarely seen on the local roads, where most traffic consisted of bicycles, and carts drawn by donkeys or horses, and the three buses per day, to and from Enniskillen and Derrylummond. One day Alfie McBrine, one of our neighbours, was driving his horse and cart out on to the road from a field adjoining our house, when a car travelling to Kinowla, collided with it. Luckily little damage was done, but when Alfie recovered from the shock, he pushed back his cap, scratched his head and said, 'Well, I've been coming out of that gate for 20 years and that's the first time that has ever happened to me!'

However the R. U. C. duly arrived and set up the screen and the projector amid great excitement, for I knew that most of the class had never seen a film. Some kind of black-out was arranged and at last the show began with a close-up picture of a man talking about crossing busy roads, but little of what he said could be heard, for once again, faced with something strange and unexpected, the children exploded into laughter, at the sight of this huge talking head. As usual they soon settled down and enjoyed the cartoons, which the police had wisely brought with them to lighten the road safety message, which was quite lost upon the children, who had never met the busy traffic conditions shown in the film. The R. U. C. never brought any films to the school again while I was there; maybe they realised the incongruity of showing such pictures in such a traffic-free area, or perhaps they did not have the resources to

visit each school more than once every 3-4 years or so. This was
a pity as it was interesting for the children to see the films, no
matter how irrelevant their content.

If the children's mental horizons were limited, so too were
their physical ones for although most of them had probably
visited Enniskillen, which was 12 miles away, few, if any, had
travelled the 90 miles to Belfast, and none had ventured
farther than that. Transport was difficult, but there seemed to
be little desire to travel even locally. Having read of the Marble
Arch, a well known limestone formation and complex of caves,
some ten miles from Kinowla, I asked John Britton how to get
to it, but he had never heard of the place, and neither had any
of our neighbours. It wasn't until a friend sent me, from
Belfast, a copy of the Ordnance Survey map, which was unob-
tainable in Enniskillen, that I was able to find the Marble Arch
and its surrounding area for myself; a pleasant bicycle ride took
me to a spot which is now one of the show places of Fermanagh,
and very well worth a visit, even by car!

A factory, making nylon stockings, had been opened in
Enniskillen in 1947, and I arranged for the older children to
be shown round it. Such visits are commonplace now, but were
unusual in 1949; a trip to the town in school time was exciting
enough but a visit to a factory was a real adventure. We were
given a warm welcome by everyone, and our tour was led by the
manager himself, who promised to give a prize for the best
essay about what we had seen. This was won by Hughie Britton,
who was given a copy of *One hundred great lives*; this was no doubt
intended as an inspirational gesture, and was received with
much enthusiasm by Hughie, but not by me, for it was a thick
tome without illustrations, and I was sure that he would not
open it, once the initial excitement was over. I cannot have
understood the Kinowla children fully, even after more than a
year with them, for Hughie treasured that book, and his family
still has it today, 41 years later. I saw it recently; it was well worn
and had obviously been put to much use, not only by Hughie,
but by his own children, who are older now than he was when
he won it. The factory disappeared many years ago, but the
book remains in use; an example perhaps of the lasting power
of literature.

When we left the nylon factory, we all went to look at the

Cole Memorial, a stone tower some 120 feet high, which was set on a hill and commanded a fine view of Enniskillen and of the surrounding countryside. Inside was a dark spiral staircase of 108 steps, leading to an open platform at the top, but, to my surprise none of the boys was willing to climb it, although all the girls did so quite happily, with many shrieks and squeals on the way. None of the children who took part in that visit went to work in that factory, but some of their successors did, which illustrates the improving state of transport during the 1950s, with people being prepared, and able, to travel over 12 miles to work.

I was not surprised to discover that hardly any of the 'scholars' had seen the sea, and as I am very fond of the sea, I thought that a trip to the seaside was an experience which all should share. Accordingly we organised a most eventful concert, the proceeds of which paid the fares of all the children, and we announced that there were a few vacant seats available for adults. To my astonishment, so many wished to come that we had to hire another coach, and on Whit Monday 1950, about 90 children and adults set out for a day at Bundoran, a seaside resort in County Donegal, some 45 miles from Kinowla.

The date was mid-May but the weather was like November, for a strong wind was blowing, heavy rain was falling from leaden skies and it was bitterly cold. Luckily, conditions improved during the day, but while it remained cold, windy and showery, nevertheless, somehow, most people enjoyed their day out, the first ever for some of them. To make matters worse, a window in one of the coaches was broken accidentally, just as we left for home, so that for its passengers even the return journey was cold and uncomfortable. My abiding memory of that much anticipated day is the sight of a group of children merrily licking ice-cream, whilst my hands were thrust deep into my pockets and my coat collar was turned up high against the rain which had just begun to fall once more. The children were happy despite everything and they had all seen the great Atlantic Ocean, so perhaps it had been worthwhile after all, although it did not seem so to me in the wind and the rain, on that bleak afternoon.

Other visits of a local nature also took place, mostly in connection with football, which was probably the most popu-

lar of all the activities at school, certainly among the boys,
although one or two of the girls played as well. At the back of
the school was a small field, which I assumed was the school
field, although I discovered later that it was in fact, the 'Master's Field, for him to use as he wished, any proceeds to be
added to his salary. Previously it had been rented annually to
a local farmer as a hayfield, but now we used it as a playground,
and a sports field, where we did Physical Education and played
games. Owing to their limited experience of games of any kind,
and ball games in particular, the children played with very
much more energy than skill, but they improved with practice,
although I always shuddered at the sight of the hob-nailed
boots in which the boys played football. I recall seeing a small
group of boys kicking away madly at each other, with the bright
hob-nails flashing, unaware that the ball had been cleared, and
was now in another part of the field! One day Charles Taylor's
father complained to me that Charles had been kicked while
he was playing football, and Mr Taylor had to be persuaded
that this was an occupational hazard, and had not been done
with malice aforethought. I must say, that this was not difficult,
although I did not tell him, as I might easily have done, that his
son's hobnails were the biggest and toughest of all, and that he
was not over-careful about whom, or what, he kicked with them!

Whilst we were learning to play football at Kinowla, other
newly arrived teachers in the area, who had become my
friends, were encouraging the game at their schools also, and
at last the great day came, when a match was arranged on our
field between Kinowla and Teelin P. E. School, from about six
miles away, the first such event of its kind ever in the district,
it appeared. In order to make up a full team of eleven players,
all the boys in my class had to be included, so that there were
no problems of selection, and no-one was upset about being
left out.

Before the day of the match, John Britton and I toured a
nearby wood and selected suitable trees for making goal-posts;
we then cut them down and erected them onto the field. The
following Saturday the boys and I carried out a useful math-
ematical exercise in marking out the pitch with sawdust, which
Peter Carr, a shopkeeper's son, had transported by horse and
cart from his home, having to be sent back twice for more

supplies, so liberal had been our application! John Britton had also supplied posts for corner flags, and Mrs Hopkins and the girls had made the actual flags, so that the entire event had been a communal effort, by all at the school. With the flags in position, the pitch was ready for the big match. It wasn't Wembley Stadium; the corners were not exactly square, and there were clumps of rushes growing all over the playing area, but we were pleased with our work and thought that we had done a good job, with the goal-posts upright and firm, the lines showing clearly and the bright yellow flags blowing in the gentle breeze.

The team had been kitted out with shirts of approximately the same colour, and Mark Britton, our goal-keeper, was resplendent in a green jersey. Teelin appeared in different colours from ours, which was fortunate for no-one had thought about a possible clash. A crowd of about 50 had gathered to watch the game, which as expected, was not a very skilful one, with much wild kicking, plenty of rushing around and lots of wasted energy and effort. The only goal of the match was scored by the Teelin outside right, whose shot for goal was well covered by Mark, until the ball struck a clump of rushes, causing it to change direction sharply and to jump back over the goal-line, leaving poor Mark helpless at the other side of the goalmouth. He was most upset and, in all future matches when he was keeping goal, he made sure that there were no rushes growing in vital positions near the posts! Despite frenzied attempts by Kinowla, they were unable to equalise, but both teams enjoyed the game so much that little importance was attached to the result, and any lingering disappointment was quickly dispelled when the teams entered the school building afterwards, for unknown to me, a group of parents had organised vast quantities of sandwiches and cakes and buns of every description, together with tea and orange juice, so that what had begun as a football match, developed into a feast, and a friendly social occasion, the forerunner of similar happy events after all other matches. Therein of course lay its value, not merely as an exercise in football, although that too was important, leading as it did much later on, to the formation of a village football team, but as an opportunity to meet strangers, to enjoy their company and to make friends with them.

The game of cricket has always been one of my abiding interests, and in my enthusiasm, I was keen that we should play it at school. As ever, equipment was an enormous problem, but from my long suffering friends and relatives, who were already supplying me with comics like 'Beano' and 'Dandy' for use during wet lunch-times, I obtained a bat and a set of stumps, so that when summer came we were ready to begin; but to my amazement and sadness, (for this was a real deprivation!), the children had never heard of the game. Upon reflection, I should not have been surprised by this, for they had no contact with cricket at all, and the nearest club was in Enniskillen; nevertheless it came as a shock when George Regan said, 'Cricket? That's a wee insect which hops over the hearth at night!'

Our attempts at the game were not successful. Most of the children used the bat as a kind of scoop, their favourite shot being a sweep to leg, played with the blade almost horizontal, and scraping the tips of the grass on the pitch. They never mastered over-arm bowling either, and only managed to bring the ball down about five yards from the bowler's end, from whence it trickled along to the batsman, who usually missed it! There were times however, when energetic action by the bowler propelled the ball high into the air, to pass over the heads of batsman, wicket keeper and long stop, and roll down to the far reaches of the field, enabling the batsmen to register more runs by means of extras, than they ever did with the bat. Yet we persevered and managed to enjoy the game, but often for the wrong reasons: it hurts me to say, that today, although they all remember the football, no-one recalls anything about cricket. Horizons could not be widened that far!

One evening Elizabeth and I were 'caileying' with our neighbours, George and May McBrine, and their daughter Vera, and I was telling them about trying to play cricket at school. With the usual twinkle in his eye George said, 'Would you like to see a cricket match?' I replied, 'Yes please', without having any idea of what was going to happen, but knowing enough about George to realise that he was going to have some gentle fun at my expense. He went out to the kitchen and came back with some breadcrumbs, which he scattered all over the stone hearth, in front of the glowing peat fire. As if by magic, from cracks between the hearthstones, from behind the high oak settle on which we were sitting, even it seemed, from the fire itself, little insects emerged, scurrying forth, with their legs and slender antennae quivering. They advanced towards the breadcrumbs which they then pushed into the crevices from whence they had come, and in no time at all, the hearth was clean again, and all the crumbs had vanished.

George laughed heartily at our astonishment. 'There you are,' he said, 'that's how we play cricket in Fermanagh! Now listen,' he went on, 'if you keep quiet you'll hear something.' Then when the talking ceased and everything was silent, except for the gentle hiss of the fire, and the bubbling of the water in the pot, we could hear the crickets, for that is what the insects were, chirping cheerfully from many places all around the fire. I had never seen or heard them before, and knew of them only through the title of Dickens' story, *The Cricket on the Hearth,* and the saying 'as merry as a cricket on the hearth': these crickets were merry enough and so was George, who once again had shown this man from the big English city, that he didn't know everything, although he was the 'Master!'

Although life at Kinowla was so placid, it was full of surprises, often because I expected too much. On the day of the Oxford and Cambridge University Boat Race in April 1949, I called at the village shop on my way home from a long walk over the hills beyond our house, and found James Morrow, the proprietor's nephew, serving behind the counter. James was a townsman from Enniskillen, and I knew that in his youth he had attended Portora Royal School there, which was an active rowing school, so I said to him, 'Hello James! Who won the Boat Race?'

He stared blankly back at me. 'Boat race!' he said, 'Boat race! What boat race?'

'I thought that Portora was a rowing school! Why the University boat race of course!' 'Oh!' replied James, 'Which university?' At that I gave up. ' Oxford and Cambridge,' I told him. 'Never heard of it,' said James, and dismissed it with a wave of his hand. 'What can I get you?' I bought a bar of chocolate and left the shop, still reeling from the thought that he had never heard of one of the major sporting events of the time, and what's more, did not want to know. I thought back to my days as a small boy in Bristol, when my friends and I were

all avid supporters of either Oxford or Cambridge, although
we had never been to either city, hardly knew what a university
was, did not know anybody who went to one, and had no
expectation of going to any university, anywhere. I did not
realise as I walked homeward, that at least eight of the 50 to 60
children at Kinowla during my time there, would attend
university or college although none of them went to Oxford or
Cambridge.

None of them went to the Royal Academy of Dramatic Art
either, although after a while we spent a lot of time on drama,
much of it after school. We had commenced by dramatising
simple poems, ballads and stories which I had read to the class;
such work was very popular with the children, but not with the
inspector of schools Mr Sampson, who apparently did not
approve of such 'frivolity.' He first visited Kinowla to see me in
July 1948, and the class performed for him their version of a
poem by Browning, of which he wrote in his report, 'The
dramatic effort is commendable, but poems of literary value
should be committed to memory.' This advice was not followed,
for though I am fond of poetry and read a great deal to the boys
and girls, I could see little point in their spending time
memorising it compulsorily, especially when they had perforce
to learn long passages from the Bible and the Prayer Book, as
part of their religious instruction programme.

In the books which we bought with the new requisition
money supplied by the County Education Authority, we found
short scripted plays, which were quickly learned and performed,
not only in school, but also at concerts given in Kinowla
Orange Hall, the only local hall available for community use.
(For these entertainments, many seats were borrowed from
the parochial hall of the Roman Catholic church, which in
turn used seats from the Orange hall, for their concert audiences.) Even after so many years, I blush to think of those
productions, although at the time we thought that they were
good, as did the audiences, who received them with much
applause and enthusiasm. At that time I was blissfully unaware
of the uses of mime and improvisation in educational drama,
and so thought that scripts were essential, and treated them
absolutely literally.

One play called for a camel, so we made one, using a coat

belonging to Elizabeth for a skin, and draping it over the unfortunate David Reed, who knelt on all-fours, and then had two pannier baskets slung across his back; it must have been most uncomfortable but David did not complain and was pleased to have been chosen to play the part. For another play a pig's head was required, and as making this was beyond the ability of the children, Elizabeth and I spent many long hours trying to make one, but all in vain. At last, in the early hours of the morning, and after much frustration, we decided to leave it until later, and send a message requesting help to our friend Graham Stevenson, the principal of Teelin School. The letter was sent to Graham with the conductor of the 9. 00 a. m. bus, which left children at our school and then went on to Teelin; on the 3. 00 p. m. bus that afternoon, there was a most realistic pig's head, made from thick card and paper, in a simple but effective manner, that had eluded all our previous efforts.

One memorable production was a dramatisation of the episode in 'Tom Sawyer', when Tom is ordered to paint the garden fence. By making the task appear highly desirable he is able to persuade his friends, not only to do the job for him, but to pay him for the privilege. One of the treasured objects which he receives is a dead rat, and in our play we used a real dead rat, as in my innocence, I had not thought to use anything else, especially as several volunteers assured me that such a corpse could be obtained easily. The performance at Kinowla went so well that we were asked to repeat it in a hall in the next parish, during another concert. With an eagerness that should have roused my suspicion, George Regan agreed to supply the rat, and duly did so.

The play received a warm welcome, and I then left for home as that concluded our part in the proceedings, but the concert was far from over. George decided that he could have some fun with the rat's body, which was tied on to a long string. He was sitting in the audience, and, I was told later, he would produce the rat whenever the action became boring. Merely to produce the body was sufficient to cause loud exclamations, but when he decided to swing it around on the string, there were so many screams and shouts, mixed with yells and raucous laughter, and so many people moving to new seats as far away from George as possible, that the concert came to a halt until George

and his rat were ejected from the hall! It was no wonder that the
rector of that parish thought that I was crazy to do such plays,
but then, he had already labelled me as a communist, because
I was in favour of the newly introduced National Health
Service. However 'Tom Sawyer Paints the Fence' was never
produced by us again.

Among the children who became most keen on performing
were the boys of the Britton family, Hughie the oldest, Mark
and Willie, who would often produce little shows for Elizabeth
and myself, when we visited their house. Mark, in particular,
was very good, and wearing an old hat of his father's, and
waving his walking stick, he would sing songs or recite poems
with great vivacity. He still maintains this interest and even yet
is in demand to do a turn at entertainments in Kinowla and
district. His younger brother, Willie, speaks warmly of our
'dramatic efforts' and tells me that they have lingered long in
the memories of those who took part, which means most of the
class, for nearly all were concerned with them in one way or
another.

I am sure however, that none will remember an experiment
in letter-writing which was a complete failure. One of my major
concerns was in ensuring that, as far as possible, all the work
done at school should have an obvious relevance for the
children, and so I reasoned that as writing letters would be one
form of written English which they would continue to use after
leaving school, we should encourage it at Kinowla. Elizabeth
had a cousin, who was the headmaster of a school in
Kaministikwa in Canada, and thinking that it would be exciting
for the childen to write to such a distant part of the world, I
arranged that his pupils and mine should write to each other.
Very quickly we realised that this would not work, as his
children were Finnish in origin, with English as their second
language, and our children found themselves unable to bridge
the immense gulf which lay between them and the Canadians.

After a while the correspondence lapsed, since it was not
satisfactory for anyone, but a happy outcome was that our
children made a 'Scrapbook of County Fermanagh,' which we
intended to send to Canada; it was not finished until long after
the last letters had been sent, and so the book was retained in
the school. I have it yet, as a potent reminder of Kinowla School

and its pupils; it has also been most useful in showing present-day children just how fortunate they are in having such good school buildings, for many of them hardly believe that the Kinowla 'scholars' were able to exist in such poor conditions.

Florence Martin wrote to the *Impartial Reporter* asking readers for material for our Scrapbook, and was thrilled when her letter was published in full in the newspaper, with its wide local circulation. She was pleased also that the Editor, no less, supported her request, and wrote that 'other schools should take note and follow the good example set by Kinowla.' Her joy was unbounded when, later that week the postman brought to the school several replies to her letter, including pictures of the county, and some specimens of tweed woven in Lisbellaw. This was the beginning of a long series of letters written by the children to various companies and organisations asking for information or catalogues or illustrations; they were interested to do this and it led to great excitement when the answers began to come in from various parts of the world. All this activity made the children's writing more real for them, and knowing that their letters would be read by strangers, was a strong incentive to neat handwriting and accurate spelling.

However, we also wrote the normal type of school essay, and on marking these, my own knowledge of English as used in Fermanagh widened considerably. I was marking a set of descriptions of the village shop and the first one said, 'Outside of the shop are some graips,' so I dutifully crossed out the last word and inserted 'grapes.' When several other essays also mentioned 'graips,' I began to wonder what they meant and reflected that it was extremely unlikely that the shop would sell grapes. Only when I asked Elizabeth, did I understand that they were not referring to fruit, but to the forks used for digging potatoes or manure, which are known as graips in Ulster, so that I had hastily to re-mark all the essays which I had corrected incorrectly.

Describing her activities during the previous day, Nellie Hamilton wrote, 'I sat down in the chair and never found until it was two o'clock.' I inserted an omission mark after 'found, and next day asked Nellie what had she been looking for. 'Nothing, said Nellie, 'I went to sleep.'

'Then why did you say that you never found something?' I

demanded. Nellie was a quiet, unassuming little girl, but she stared at me, and said in what was for her, almost an aggressive tone, 'I said I went to sleep. I never found, means that I went to sleep.' We were able to laugh together at my ignorance, but I had a private smile at another essay which read 'I washed my hands and face and behind', only to read, 'my ears' on the next page!

I always regretted being unable to do more than I did to interest the children in music. As a brand-new teacher straight from college, I agreed readily with Mrs Hopkins' suggestion that she should continue to teach music to all the school as, she assured me, she had done for many years. Very soon I realised that I had made a mistake, for the music lessons consisted of singing the first song in the tattered song-book, then proceeding to the second, then the third and so on, omitting the Christmas carols, until the half-hour lesson was over! Because of this I renewed acquaintance with some old favourites such as *The ash grove, All through the night, Billy Boy* and *Blow away the morning dew,* but I do not recall ever going as far as *Come lassies and lads.* Mrs Hopkins worked hard, and I was reluctant to upset her by offering to take the singing myself, which might have been an improvement, but only, I think, in the repertoire. I could have used the singing lessons from the radio, as I did in my next school, and now I cannot think why I did not do so, as they were excellent for non-music readers like me. However, I did try using some broadcast lessons in the appreciation of music but they were too advanced for our children, especially as it was impossible to do any follow-up work, since at that time there were no battery operated record players. Unfortunately then, little music was taught at Kinowla, but were I to teach there now, it would have an important place in the curriculum.

We did some work in art and craft, chiefly painting and drawing, with needlework for the girls and model-making for the boys, although the girls joined in when models were needed for geography and other lessons. A few years earlier, during the Second World War, the then Principal had taught the boys to knit socks for themselves; this was a most progressive move, which had lapsed when Mrs Gracey left, and I was certainly unable to revive it! The standard of art work was not high and as my own artistic ability is almost non-existent, I was able to do little to help, except to provide ideas and encouragement, but perhaps for that reason, the pictures and patterns were dull and uninteresting, and not the bright, lively and uninhibited displays of colour for which I had hoped.

In January 1949, when I had been teaching for a year, we had just finished a picture-making session, the children had gone home and I was collecting the paintings which they had left to dry. I gathered them up, and there, at the top of the pile was Pauline Taylor's painting, a drab daub, which to me was just a mess. 'Look at that,' I thought to myself, 'isn't that ghastly? What good am I doing here if that is the best which a girl like Pauline can do?'

I was tempted to tear up the picture with all its blotches and streaks, but I refrained from doing so and looked through the entire collection. This only increased my frustration for, to my, by now, jaundiced eyes, there wasn't a single piece of good work among them. Feeling dis-spirited and bad tempered, I thrust the twenty or so paintings on top of the pile of pictures, which was on a shelf in the cupboard, and clumsily managed to knock them all to the floor. Angrily I began to pick up the pieces of curling paper, among them a picture which was even worse than the one by Pauline which had so upset me, and I turned it over to see who had executed this monstrosity. On the back was written, 'Pauline Taylor. March 3rd, 1948.' and my spirits leapt up again, for when I put the two pictures together, poor though they both were, the improvement shown in the later work was obvious. I sorted out some other paintings, and in almost every case there was some evidence of progress; clearly something was being achieved so that perhaps all my work had not been in vain after all.

A little, late wintry sunshine filtered through the tiny windows of the school as I put away the paintings for the second time, but they had taught me a lesson about teaching which I have never forgotten; it is the relative improvement in the child's own attainments which is important, and not just the absolute standard which is achieved. If the children are performing to the best of their ability, that is all we can ask of them, even if their achievements are not very high; I learned that from Pauline Taylor's paintings and have been re-assured by it throughout my teaching career. Various ministers of education do not seem to know that, with their insistence on common standards, but then, they were not taught by Pauline Taylor!

That evening I went home feeling very happy, for until then, I had not considered that I was doing much good at Kinowla; it was frustrating to find the children needing so much when I could give them so little. I was anxious for results, but they were slow in coming, and I failed to realise that the results I sought would come only in the long term; this was a philosophical attitude which eluded me for a long time. I once described teaching at Kinowla as being like banging my head against a brick wall, without the physical pain, but because of Pauline's pictures, that wall now appeared to be a little less solid! At last I was on the way to becoming a real teacher.

A great obstacle to progress at school was the poor attendance of many of the children, who remained at home for the slightest of reasons. It was true that some of them had long distances to walk to school; a few came on the bus, but they also had a long journey to the bus stop. In bad weather, parents were reluctant to send their children out, knowing that their clothes would be soaked and that there was no way of drying them at Kinowla, yet still I thought that attendance might be improved.

One day a man entered the schoolroom without knocking, and walked across to me, seeming most familiar with his surroundings. In his rough tweed jacket and trousers, and without a tie, he looked like a farmer just about to start work. He took off his cap, shook hands with me and said, in a soft Fermanagh accent, 'Good morning, Master, I'm Mr Regan.' 'He's the father of Jim and George,' I thought. 'I wonder what he wants? At least he told me who he is, but he might have knocked.' 'How are the boys attending?' he went on, somewhat ill at ease, yet obviously used to the school.'Very well,' I responded, 'they hardly miss a day.' but I wondered why he didn't know that for himself. Maybe he suspected them of playing truant. 'And they're always early,' I added, for Jim and George were always regular and punctual in attendance.

A long pause followed; then Mr Regan asked to see the attendance register. Why should a parent want to see the register? Perhaps he didn't believe me and wanted to check the boys' attendance for himself. I opened the book for him, and watched, as he ran his finger down all the names on the roll, and then looked at the attendances shown against each one. He did this with a practised hand, and I began to have an idea of who he might be. He took out a small black book, into which he wrote the names of two children, who were often absent from school, before closing the register and turning to me once more.

'I'll call and see about these two,' he said, putting the book into his pocket and placing his cap on his head. 'Thank you very much Master.' I still wondered what he meant, but didn't ask him. All I said was 'Thank you. Good morning, Mr Regan.' He was very puzzled. 'Regan?' he said, 'My name's not Regan, I'm Mr Fagan, the Attendance Officer. I'll be back to see you soon.' and with that he touched his cap and went out. I never saw Mr Fagan again, and never knew if he did go to see the two children, whose names he had entered in his little black book.

Little by little, attendance began to improve, perhaps due to Mr Fagan's efforts, but also possibly because the children appeared to like school more than before, and were more interested in the work which we were doing together, now that we knew and understood each other better. Mr Sampson carried out another inspection of the school in July 1949 and reported that, 'The children are thoroughly enjoying their school life,' and I like to think that that is why the average attendance improved from 69% in 1947 to 92% in the year ending September 1950, which was when I left Kinowla.

Some time before then, a neighbour said to Elizabeth, 'I don't know what goes on at your husband's school, but I was in a house this morning and the children were making a terrible fuss because they couldn't go to school. It wasn't like that in my time. We cried because we had to go to school, but they were crying because they couldn't go. I've never heard of that before!' Perhaps I was doing some good after all.

5 At Home

AFTER SCHOOL each day I packed into my bag the exercise books which had to be marked that night and cycled toward Derrylummond for about a mile, crossing the Claddagh river on the way, before I reached Carrick Cottage which had become our home. It was on the right hand side of the road and below the road level; two steps led down into a small front garden, with a path up to the green door. The walls were whitewashed and on sunny days the yellow thatch gleamed, since the straw had recently been renewed. Carrick was always warm and welcoming, we had painted its door and window frames in bright colours so that it was never dull, even on the darkest of days.

Inside there were two bedrooms, a living room and a kitchen, and it was very different from any house in which either of us had lived before coming to Kinowla. There was no electricity, no piped water supply, and our food was cooked on a black coal-burning range or on Primus stoves; lighting was by oil lamps, and water had to be fetched from the stream at the other side of the road or from the famous spring-well across two fields. Each morning the Primus had to be lit to boil water for tea or for washing, before the range was cleaned out and re-lit, using sticks and coal, to provide a fire for cooking and to heat the house. Each night the lamp was filled with paraffin oil and its wicks trimmed before they were lit, to spread the soft glow of lamplight around the room. Later on we obtained an Aladdin lamp, which was magic indeed, as it had a mantle instead of wicks, and gave an intense white light, very much brighter but very much less pleasant than the older lamps. Sometimes soot would gather on the mantle, and would catch fire, enveloping the lamp and its glass chimney in tall tongues of flame. Once these were extinguished by turning down the light, salt had to be spread on the mantle to burn off the soot, and the chimney also had to be cleaned, for it too would be blackened. Despite these almost nightly incidents, the Aladdin's light was so much brighter, and illuminated so much more of the room, that it gradually replaced the simpler, earlier lamps, yet I was sorry to see them go, for they gave a perfect light for marking books!

With the curtains drawn, a clear fire burning in the range and the oil lamp shedding its gentle radiance around, our living room was warm and cosy and attractive, even on the coldest of winter evenings. It was attractive in summer also, when it was fresh and cool, and never more so than one June evening when we were expecting some visitors from Belfast to arrive at about ten ò'clock. Elizabeth had prepared the table, using a newly starched and embroidered cloth, the late sunshine was still streaming through the open window, its rays reflected by the cutlery and dishes, and adding a sparkle to the glow of a golden evening.

When all was ready, we sat on the low bridge outside the house enjoying the warm air, the scent of the flowers and the sounds of the birds until, tired of waiting, I said that I would go in to make a cup of tea. Elizabeth didn't want any, but warned me very strictly to make sure that I did not spill anything on the new white cloth. I made the tea without mishap and brought it outside, to enjoy it in the light of the setting sun, which filled the sky with every possible shade of crimson.

Elizabeth changed her mind and went in to make tea for herself, while I sat on the warm stones of the bridge, admiring the sunset and listening to the rippling of the water. Suddenly a loud cry came from inside the house. I dashed in to find that Elizabeth had done the very thing that she had warned me to avoid; her tea had been spilled over the table, and was lying in shallow pools upon the cloth. As usual, right away she spotted the best thing to do. 'Clear the table quickly!' she commanded, and we did just that, to find, as she had hoped, that the top cloth had been starched so stiffly that the liquid had not gone through it, and the cloth beneath had not been touched at all. We were able to re-set the table upon this second cloth, and had just completed our renewed preparations, when a car drew up outside and our visitors were at the door.

It was their first visit to Carrick Cottage and they fell under its spell at once. 'What a lovely room!,' they said, 'Everything looks so fresh and bright. And what a beautiful table!' Elizabeth and I smiled at each other but made no comment; the only evidence of our mishap was the once starched cloth, and it was out of sight, lying limply in a bowl of cold water in a corner of the kitchen.

Both Elizabeth and I had lived all our lives in big cities, in houses with many devices for making life easier, and at first we found living in such a basic cottage very trying, but gradually we became accustomed to all the extra tasks involved, and at last came to regard them as normal. There were many compensations though, but not in the back garden, which had been untended for many years and was now an un-reclaimable wilderness, except for some gooseberry and blackberry bushes which despite their long neglect, continued to bear delicious berries every summer. Beyond the hedges were the meadows, never cultivated, but used each year for hay, so that in early summer they became bright with the tall lances of green grass before being cut, when the rounded mounds of hay were dotted around like low golden hills. After a while came the aftergrass. a sea of emerald green, gleaming brightly around the yellowing islands of the tiny haystacks.

Before hay-time came, the grass was starred with buttercups, daisies and many other wild flowers including several varieties of orchid, hitherto unheard of by me, but now a source of great delight with their yellow, cream and purple spikes forming splashes of colour amid the green waves of the grass. To saunter across the fields to the well on a sunny summer evening was a pleasure, even though two heavy buckets filled with water had to be carried back, but on wet days, or in winter, when the soil was water-logged, it was far from pleasant, and water-carrying then was just a chore to be endured.

Our surroundings were a source of constant joy to us and, in those days of little mechanical traffic, so peaceful, with little sound save for the birds and the wind, the stream, and the rumble of an occasional horse and cart passing by on the road. The silence was so vital that it could almost be touched, it was folded around us with such a hushed intensity that it seemed to have a physical presence of its own. It was a living atmosphere spread over the fields and hills like the mothering ways of a hen over her eggs, making everything feel secure, protected and at peace. To turn from the main road, just two miles away, was to enter this world of stillness, a wonderful feeling which haunts my memory even yet.

A less romantic view of hens was taken by the farmers' wives, who were responsible for them and for rearing the turkeys at Christmas; the hens and at the right time, their chicks, wandered freely through every farmyard, and made a fascinating sight as, in their feathers of every hue; white, black and the burnished copper of the Rhode Island Reds, they stalked around, scattering only when a strange cat or dog disturbed them, and they dispersed rapidly in a cloud of whirring wings and frightened clamour. Elizabeth once expressed an interest in rearing some day-old chicks, and Vera McBrine encouraged her. 'If you buy the chicks,' she said, 'I'll lend you a hoover.' This baffled Elizabeth. How could a vacuum cleaner be of use in rearing chicks, and in any case there was no electricity as Vera knew well. Was it just one of the jokes which Vera'a father loved to play on us?

'What good will that be?' she asked. 'I have a vacuum cleaner of my own, but it's no use to us here.' Vera laughed. 'I don't mean a cleaner. A hoover is used to keep young chicks in, until they are big enough to run around outside.' and she took Elizabeth to see the hoover, a metal incubator about three feet square, in which a flock of fluffy yellow chicks was cheeping and running around. Later we discovered that the spelling of that kind of hoover is 'hover', and interestingly enough, an eight-eenth century sense of the verb to hover is 'to cover young birds with wings and body', which is exactly what the hover does for the chicks. It would seem that hover is one of the many words still used in Northern Ireland in their original sense, although they have lost it elsewhere.

At the side of Carrick Cottage was a path which at first followed a stream, but later left it to head up into the hills, and eventually to the heathery slopes of Mullagh Mountain, which was some 1800 feet high. Below its rounded summit was a waterfall about 50 feet high, which was a dramatic sight after heavy rainfall, with the river cascading in a torrent over the rocky ledge, to dash into the deep pool far below. Few people ever went to see it, possibly because of its remoteness, but more likely because, when it was at its most spectacular, the approaches were difficult as the surrounding peat bogs were so wet. Nevertheless I went to visit it one day, and was certain that I had seen no-one around, yet months later, when I was in Kinowla I was asked if I had been walking on Mullagh again since that day!

Nearer the house, however, and before it reached the open hillside, the path rose steeply between high hedges of hawthorn and hazel, which were laden with nuts in autumn; in summer creamy honeysuckle climbed with splendid abandon all through the hedges, filling the soft air with its perfume, mingling with a sharper scent from a line of tall lime trees, which shaded a plateau of high green grass, where once a house had stood. Now only the ruined walls were left, their grey stones lying unevenly and coated with moss and lichen; a spot at which to pause for breath, but also to ponder upon the people who had once lived there, and to wonder what had happened to them. It was a steep climb to their house, but they had a wonderful view from it, and its memory must have remained with them wherever they settled. It was green and pleasant there now, yet it had an air of sadness, the melancholy of a place once lively with happy voices, but now silent and deserted.

Just as those people must have done, many years before, our visitors toiled up that path, so concentrating on their climb that they did not look beyond the enclosing hedgerows, until arriving at that flat green shelf, they would pause for breath, and at last turn round, to look back down the hill. I had not told them what to expect so they were always surprised at the view. Beyond the steeply descending path with its flowers and trees, was the chequered pattern of flat green fields, and beyond them, the length of Upper Lough Erne, its shining water studded with wooded islands - 365 of them I was told, but I never bothered to count them, for the scene was so magnificent that nothing mattered except the enjoyment of its beauty. Even the least energetic of our friends, who needed much coaxing to walk at all, thought the view well worth the effort they had made to see it. But no amount of coaxing would persuade them to go beyond that oasis of green to where the path stretched upwards to Pat Malone's cottage. There, reaching the heather, it disappeared among the bog cotton and the ling, where the stillness was broken only by the cry of the curlew. All around were the gentle slopes of the hills, their rough grasses swaying in the wind, and above it all, would sometimes come that immense call, its rounded notes bubbling and spreading into a great cry of desolation, matching the loneliness of the empty landscape beneath the circling bird.

Each day, when weather and light permitted, I would walk up the path, usually for sheer pleasure, but at least once a week, in order to gather kindling for the fire, and always I was accompanied by Oscar, our dog, who would bound on ahead of me, his nose alert to every scent from the hedges, his tail waving high in the air. Looking at him when he was fully grown, I would recall his first venture up the hill, when, as a fat litle pup, he was unable to complete the full journey and had to be carried for most of the homeward descent. He was a big sheep dog, all black except for a white blaze on his chest; because of his size he was known by everyone as 'The Calf.' None of our neighbours fed their dogs as well as we fed Oscar, as was clear from their 'lean and hungry looks.' They were working dogs, too busy to put on weight, whilst Oscar led a life of ease, only taking exercise when he wished to do so, which was quite often, but, apart from our walks together, entirely at his own volition. Other dogs appeared at our door often, especially when it was feeding time for Oscar!

He had come to us one night soon after our arrival in Kinowla, when Elizabeth had cycled over to see Margaret Davey at the rectory, and I was to join her there, when I had finished my school work. The room was most comfortable, and the pile of exercise books to be marked was gradually decreasing, when there was a knock at the door. I opened it, to find Helen Kennedy, one of the older girls at the school, standing outside with what looked like a parcel under her arm. 'Please sir, I've brought the pup,' she said in answer to my greeting.

'Pup? What pup, Helen?' I replied in surprise. Helen was embarrassed by my puzzled tone and stammered, 'Mrs Claypole said to Daddy that you would take it,' and then I remembered that Elizabeth had mentioned a pup to me, but I had forgotten all about it.

'Yes of course, Helen, now I remember. We'll be pleased to

have it. But where is the pup?' 'It's here,' she said, and taking
from beneath her arm, the supposed parcel, which was now
revealed as a shopping bag, she opened it. Out waddled a
plump black puppy, which, on spotting the open door and the
warm fire beyond it, walked slowly into the living room,
stretched himself in front of the fire and promptly went to
sleep! We both laughed at his cheek as Helen called it,
although I thought of it as enterprise! 'That settles the matter,
doesn't it, Helen?' I smiled. 'He certainly means to stay here,
so we'll have to keep him now.' By this time Helen had
recovered her confidence, and when I think back to it, to come
on a pitch black night, and all alone, to the home of the new
Master, whom she hardly knew as yet, must have been quite a
trial for her.

'He'll be a good dog,' she told me, and seemed pleased and
proud that he had made such a favourable impression. We had
a cup of tea together, before Helen set off on her bike to ride
home in the darkness, but the puppy remained fast asleep until
I finished the remainder of my marking. As I put the books
away, he awoke and began to explore his new surroundings,
which apparently pleased him, for, his survey completed, he
resumed his place at the fire, and watched me carefully as I
made ready to go for Elizabeth. I picked him up and took him
out to a hayshed where there was plenty of warm hay, but he
made such an outcry, that I brought him back into the house,
where he would not rest content until he was back in his, by
now, accustomed place at the fire.

'Very well,' I said to myself, and left him to stay there until
I came back with Elizabeth, who was very keen to hurry
home when she heard of what had happened during her
absence. Some of her enthusiasm disappeared however
upon our arrival, when she saw what the pup had done whilst
we were away! A comfortable bed was made for him in the
outhouse, with some encouraging words to accompany a bowl
of warm milk; the last we saw of him that night was a tail wagging
happily as he lapped up the milk amid contented noises. If he
made more noise during the night, we were far enough away
not to hear him! Ever afterwards he slept in the shed, although
on some evenings he was allowed in the house, but when we
said 'Bed Oscar!,' he would look round appealingly, then

realising that this was in vain, he would rise very slowly and slink reluctantly to his bed among the hay.

In my formative years in a boys' club in Bristol we used Oscar as an affectionate name for anything strange, after an act performed by one of the boys, with an imaginary performing flea called Oscar; when the pup first appeared he was certainly strange and as we quickly grew fond of him, Oscar seemed an appropriate name, recalling as it did, so many happy days with my boyhood friends. Rapidly he became very well-known and most popular, so that when we went away on holiday, many people were anxious to look after him for us, but we always left him with Florence and William Martin, who lived on a farm, where there was plenty of room, and who we knew would care well for him. When he was with them, Oscar had to work for a living, for he helped the Martins with their cattle, bringing then in for milking and taking them out to the fields again; they had soon discovered that he could do this with skill, and seemed to enjoy it. Nevertheless, Oscar was delighted when we returned. and never failed to greet us with vigorous enthusiasm, jumping about and barking loudly, well aware of the fuss which we would make of him.

Yet this was nothing compared with the reception which he received from the children when he decided to visit the school. Oscar first announced his presence at Kinowla one afternoon when the children in my class were busy painting, whilst from Mrs Hopkins' end of the room came the drone of children reading to her. Suddenly there came a tremendous thump at the door, as if a large sack of potatoes had been thrown against it, then another and another. I was at the far end of the room so I asked Bobby Harvey if he would please see what was creating such a commotion. Bobby was a sturdy boy, but as he opened the door, he was almost knocked over by a bounding black bundle, which burst into the room, and ran wildly up and down among the long desks, amid cries of surprise from the children and some alarm from Mrs Hopkins, until, finding me, it jumped up excitedly, trying to put its paws up on my shoulders, barking loudly as it did so. The black bundle was Oscar, and upon his entry all work ceased, for this was something much more interesting; there had never been a dog in Kinowla School before! I tried to persuade him to wait outside but in vain, for each time he was put out, he forced his way in again, with the children making little attempt to prevent him. Finally I allowed him to remain and he spent the rest of the afternoon sitting quietly under my table.

During the next hour or so, a record number of pencils had to be sharpened, painting water was changed constantly, an unusually large number of pieces of paper had to be obtained from my desk; and scraps for the waste paper basket under my desk were legion, as all these activities enabled Oscar to be patted and stroked, to add some excitement to a quiet school afternoon. Mrs Hopkins' children were jealous, as there was no reason for them to visit the Master's end, to add their greetings to the unexpected visitor, who was revelling in the attention being given to him. He just lay under the table in great content as he received the admiration of so many children, like some Oriental potentate, reclining on a divan, and enjoying the fawning adulation of his courtiers.

Oscar was an intelligent dog, and quickly realised that such a reception was his for the asking any time he cared to come to school, whilst the children, always ready for some diversion from everyday affairs, greeted his arrival enthusiastically, so that in future, whenever a solid bang was heard at the door, someone always wanted to go out to the toilet, in order to admit Oscar, whom they knew would be waiting outside. He soon developed a routine of running up and down among the desks before going straight to my table, to lie there quietly and comfortably, and to await the homage of his loyal subjects. He seemed to be sensible enough to realise that if his appearances were too frequent, then they would not be welcomed, so that he did not come often enough to be a nuisance. His visits were appreciated by everyone, although I shudder to think of Mr Sampson, the inspector's, reaction if they had both come to the school at the same time. Maybe Oscar would have diverted him also!

Except for the days when he came to school, no matter what he had been doing earlier, Oscar would always be at Carrick Cottage to greet me upom my arrival from school. Without any warning from Elizabeth, each day at my usual home-coming time, he would wander out, and lie down in the road just outside the gate, on a long straight stretch, where oncoming traffic was visible from some distance away, almost to the cross-roads.

Soon after I had passed Kinowla Cross, as it was called, Oscar would spot me, and springing quickly to his feet, would dash off at full speed, pulling up sharply when he reached me. He would circle excitedly around my bike, and then rush off towards the house, looking backwards at intervals to ensure that I was following him safely. Once we were at home, I would give him the piece of my lunch which I kept for him each day, and then he would rest content until it was time for us to go for our evening stroll up the hill.

Ultimately however there was to be another claimant to Oscar's throne as ruler of Carrick Cottage, a smaller but equally intelligent and even more active challenger, with whom, nonetheless, he soon struck up a happy relationship, so that they were content to reign together as king and consort. During our time at Carrick Cottage we had three different cats, each named Yorick, and all of them bright and lively, but none more so than Yorick 3rd, with whom Oscar shared his sovereignty. Yorick 1st and Yorick 2nd each stayed with us for a short time only, before, we think, wandering off and becoming lost on the hills, or finding another home, but Yorick 3rd was with us for more than a year, and in that time, made a considerable impression upon our home, and upon Oscar.

She was a grey tortoiseshell kitten with lovely green eyes and a white nose; her movements were nimble and sprightly, but she was extremely fastidious and never liked to be wet or dirty. When she realised that Oscar waited for me each day, she did so also, but she sat upon a wide gate-post adjoining the house, where she would remain aloof from any wild display of affection until I had reached home. Only then would she deign to descend from her perch, stalk in her most dignified manner across to where I stood with the dog, and rub herself against my legs purring as she did so. When I had paid my respects by picking her up, stroking her fur and speaking to her in my most flattering voice, she would jump down lightly, and with regal steps, walk off to resume her queenly pursuits.

Yorick 3rd hated the rain and would not venture out to meet me on wet days; however on days when no rain was falling but the top of the gate-post was damp, she would saunter forth and sit on top of Oscar as he lay in the road, and with great hauteur, would survey the passing scene from her soft and lofty throne. The dog did not object to this burden, but as soon as he saw me, he would shrug Yorick from his back with a sudden flick, and set off down the road to meet me, leaving the cat to find a dry spot of her own.

He was a good natured animal and shared a dish of milk with Yorick without demur, and would even allow her to play tricks on him. We had an old rocking chair with slats of wood at its back; we kept it in the outhouse and Oscar liked to sit in it, with his long tail protruding through the bars at one side as, curled up in the seat, he snoozed quietly and contentedly. But not for long, for if Yorick should appear, as she often did, on seeing him in the chair, her eyes would dance with mischief and she would tug at his tail from behind his back, and then run over to the opposite side. The dog would turn in the chair to discover the cause of this annoyance, and his tail would then hang down on the other side, just as Yorick knew it would; whereupon she would pull it again and run once more to the far side, so that she could give a repeat performance.

Tolerant as ever, Oscar would usually oblige, but he would never allow his tail to be pulled for more than three times, for after that, as if to say, 'Enough's enough. You've had your fun for today,' he would draw it in, curl up in the chair with the tail wrapped securely around him, and go to sleep again, ignoring with utter disdain, all Yorick's attempts to play with him. He too could show scorn, even towards such a royal kitten as Yorick!

Yorick 3rd was a truly beautiful kitten, and was extremely popular with our neighbour, Mary O'Neill, who looked after her for us when we were away. The kitten was well on the way to being a cat, for she was more than a year old, when upon our return from a short holiday, Mary told us that Yorick had not come to be fed the previous evening, and she had not seen her all that day either .. we never saw Yorick again and were most upset at the loss. Mary thought that she had been stolen, for she was so attractive that a passer-by might easily have been tempted to take her; a cat would always be useful around the house in the country, and her good looks would be a bonus. Oscar went on as ever; he and Yorick had been such good friends that we wondered if he missed her, but he showed no signs of doing so.

We certainly did, but decided that as this was the third kitten which we had lost, we would not have another. 'Alas poor Yorick,' she was the last of her line for us.

The dog continued to thrive, and stayed with us throughout the remainder of our time at Kinowla, a constant friend and companion. After nearly three years had passed we were to leave Fermanagh altogether, and Elizabeth and I found it difficult to decide to take him with us, much as we wanted to do so, for our new home was at the side of a busy road, and in sheep-rearing country. Oscar had never seen a sheep and we were fearful about sheep-worrying; and how would a dog, who was used to lying in the middle of the road waiting for me, react to a road where traffic was relatively constant? Yet we could not bear the thought of leaving him, although the Martins would gladly give him a good home, and the same companionship which he had known with us. Finally we allowed our hearts to over-rule our heads, and made up our minds to take him with us; the Martins were saddened by this but resigned themselves to it.

However on the night before we left Kinowla, Oscar did not come home; this was the first time he had failed to do so and we could not find him anywhere. Next morning the removal van arrived and was loaded with furniture; we were ready and there was still no sign of Oscar. When we could wait no longer we set off, leaving a message with Mary O'Neill that if he should turn up, Oscar was to be taken to the Martin's farm, making a sad leave-taking even more sad. When we reached Kinowla Cross, there stood P. C. Parke, who raised his hand to stop us. 'Aren't you taking your big black dog with you?' he enquired.

'We were,' I answered, 'but he didn't come home last night, and we've not seen him today.'

'Well he's in the village outside Charlie Morris's shop. Do youwant me to fetch him for you?'

Elizabeth and I looked at each other and agonised over what we should do. Without saying a word, we went over all our earlier discussions and recalled our many doubts; perhaps our decision to take Oscar had been a selfish one, for would he be as happy in his new home as he was now?

Time seemed to stand still, although I was aware of the drumming of the lorry-driver's fingers on the steering wheel, for we were already late, and had a long journey ahead of us. At last I looked at Elizabeth, but said nothing; as if reading my thoughts, she nodded her head, and I understood that her decision was the same as mine. I swallowed hard, took a deep breath, and said to the constable, 'Will you get him for me please, and take him down to the Martins at Lisfern. They'll be glad to have him and will give him a good home.' 'Of course,' replied the constable, 'I'll do that just as soon as I get back to the village. But aren't you going to miss him?' Doubts came flooding back, and for a second of eternity, I was tempted once more. That second however was just a pause in the policeman's reply. 'Goodbye,' he went on, 'and good luck!' He raised his hand in salute, the driver started the engine and we turned towards Teelin Bridge and the main road. Elizabeth and I were silent, not daring to speak, for that would reveal the depth of our emotions. We knew that we had done the right thing but could not help feeling sad about it, for leaving Oscar behind, or deserting him as it appeared to me, was scant reward for his loyalty and devotion, and for all the pleasure and happiness which he had given us. But then we saw James Boyce, whose big smile and cheery wave did much to restore our drooping spirits. They were soon raised even higher, for we had not been long in our new home before it was plain that Oscar would not have been happy there; with so many sheep in the fields, and lots of cars on the road, we could not have allowed him the freedom to roam, to which he had been accustomed, and his life would have been miserable.

A year passed and we went back to Kinowla to stay with some friends who lived at Fernagh, about three miles from the village, and one and a half miles from the Martin's farm, which was between the two, but at the end of a long lane which led from the road to the farmhouse. On Sunday evening we went to church and after the service came down the steps to the road, with the rest of the congregation. It was very dark, and suddenly I felt something brush against me, two paws appeared on my shoulders, and amid whimpers of joy, a rough tongue licked my cheek, – it was Oscar, who somehow had sensed our presence over so much time and distance, and had sought us out. It was a very emotional reunion, which brought much warmth and joy to all three of us, but when the euphoria had died down a little, we looked round for the Martins to take Oscar home with them. There was no sign of them, so we took him to Lisfern ourselves, and they were most surprised to see us, having had no idea that we were back again, as we had neither told them of our visit, nor gone to see them, for fear of upsetting Oscar... and ourselves! They had not been to church that evening, and so Oscar must have made his own way there, although William assured me that he had never left the farm before. We were all amazed at what had happened, but happy too, and none happier than Oscar, who spent the rest of the time running between Elizabeth and myself, lying beside each of us for a while, and then scampering off, with tail held high, to seek the attention of the other. After that evening of intense feeling, we never saw Oscar again.

For some years we heard about him from time to time, until the Martins left Fermanagh themselves; they then gave the dog to a friend who was a postman in a village some five miles from Kinowla, with whom we had no contact, although we were told that Oscar accompanied him on his rounds. I'm sure that Oscar's tail was still held erect, and I can picture him, with his tongue curved between his teeth as he turned his head, and lifted his dark eyes as if to say, as he had done so many, many times to me on that hillside path, 'Come on, there's much more to see along here. I'll show you the way!'

6 Around and About

From *The Importance of Being Earnest*, Act Three, by Oscar Wilde:

> *JACK: I have also, in my possession, certificates of Miss Cardew's birth, baptism, whooping cough, registration, vaccination, confirmation, and the measles; both the German and the English variety.*
> *LADY BRACKNELL: Ah! A life crowded with incident, I see!*

SO TOO was our life in Kinowla. There was more to it than school and enjoying the countryside, and time passed very quickly, for even if nothing was happening, there were always visits to make, and we never knew from one day to the next, who would come to see us that evening. If most of the incidents in our life were just about as dramatic as those in Cecily Cardew's, they were certainly more numerous, for we often went to 'cailey' with our neighbours, when all sorts of things might occur! Originally the word 'ceilidhe' meant an informal dance, but in Fermanagh during our time there, it had come to mean also, calling on people for a chat. Because of this custom, anyone was likely to call upon anyone else, which was a great help in breaking down social barriers, although few existed around Kinowla, where there were no wealthy people, and everyone mixed readily.

If at any time we were at a loss for something to do, we could always go for a cailey to the Brittons or the McBrines or the O'Neills, or maybe a knock would come at the door and 'God bless all here' would herald the arrival of Joe O'Neill, or Peter Malone, who had come for a night's good 'crack,' as a lively chat is known in Ulster. They would rarely leave before the early hours of the morning, for the inhabitants of the country-

68

side around us were not early risers, although in my urban
ignorance I had thought that farmers everywhere rose with the
lark! The creamery lorry did not call for the milk until late in
the morning, so that, in winter especially, no-one bothered too
much about time, and the truth of John Britton's statement
about plenty of time having been created, very soon made itself
evident to me. School did not begin until 9.30. a.m. and even
so, some children were often late, not only because they had a
long distance to walk, but also because, if they did not make a
nuisance of themselves, they were allowed to sit up whilst the
adults had their crack, so that they often 'slept in.'

Since many of these visits involved a journey of several miles,
and none of our friends except Brian Davey owned a car, we
found ourselves making frequent use of the bicycles, which we
had bought soon after arriving in Fermanagh. They were our
usual means of transport, and were used to carry everything
from groceries to day-old chicks. We often found ourselves
cycling home long after midnight, and on one occasion rode
into the middle of an unexpected flood in Derrylummond at
2.00 a.m. Even now I can feel the bitterly cold water lapping
round my ankles as I struggled to push the bike through the
pool, which covered the road. Brian Davey's car would have
been welcome then. It was an old Ford Eight, and sometimes
he would tie Elizabeth's bike across the back of the car and
bring her home in style, but all this ceased when the Ford
became so unreliable that it had to be changed.

Its replacement was a brand-new, shining-black Morris Minor, of which Brian was rightly proud; no bike could be allowed
to sully its gleaming paintwork, and so Elizabeth now had to
cycle home from the rectory. I had never ridden in a new car
before, and travelling in the Minor was an experience to
savour, for it was like riding on air, with the car humming
quietly along, smoothly and serenely, even on the bumpy roads
around Skenbarra. Although it was a long time before a bike
was tied to it, Brian's car was soon in use for the multitude of
purposes for which a car is used in the country, especially if it
belongs to a helpful rector, which Brian Davey certainly was.
He seemed to provide a general delivery service in his parish,
taking small animals to the vet., collecting parcels from
Enniskillen, and transporting parishioners and goods to church

events. The rector's car was a carrier's van, a bus, a taxi and an ambulance all combined! It would have been used too much for it to survive until the late 1980s, and become a collector's item, as have some of its contemporaries, to be cleaned and polished and coddled like children.

Anyone coming from Belfast by train and bus to visit us, had to be prepared to cycle the two and a half miles from Teelin Bridge, as this was the nearest stop to Carrick Cottage for the bus from Enniskillen, which connected with the train from Belfast. I would go to meet the visitor there, riding my own bike with my left hand on its handlebars, and using my right hand to steer a second machine, which wobbled along beside me, and was intended for the visitor's use. Somehow I never managed to finish in the ditch, although my progress was always precarious, and filled with anxiety, especially if I chanced to meet a car or a tractor on the narrow bog road, which led to the main highway. The return journey was equally unsteady, for then, although relieved of the second bike, I had to ride with a large suitcase resting on the handlebars, and between my knees. It was always a relief to reach home without mishap! If we went to Enniskillen for the day, we would ride the bikes to the bus stop, and leave them in a hedge of the nearest field, knowing that when we returned some hours later, they would still be lying there, untouched, just as our milk could be left in perfect safety at the cross-roads, half a mile from the house.

We cycled for fun also and enjoyed exploring much of the countryside to the south of Upper Lough Erne, sometimes venturing as far as Cavan, although this meant running the gauntlet of a flock of geese, which patrolled the road near the border. When an unsuspecting cyclist approached, the geese would rush out with their long necks extended, their beaks opening wide as they uttered fierce cries in support of their attacks. Surrounded by flapping wings, vicious beaks and wild eyes in a whirlwind of din, all that the cyclist could do was to put his head down and pedal as fast as he could through the noisy aggressors; no-one was hurt by the geese however, so that perhaps they were not as dangerous as they seemed. Cycling on to Cavan after surviving the raid, I was reminded of how Rome had been saved when the honking of geese had aroused its sleeping defenders in time to ward off a sudden attack, and I had no trouble in believing the story, for I was sure that the bellicose screaming, which I had just endured, must have been heard well beyond the Seven Hills!

When I look back after so many years, it seems strange to me that Upper Lough Erne should play such a small part in my recollections, for I am certain that if I lived in Kinowla now, much of my time would be spent around the lake, enjoying the beauties of landscape, water and skies, and observing the wild life, especially the birds, of the Lough.

In those far off-days Lough Erne was like an awe-inspiring friend, whom one didn't visit too often, although being assured of a warm welcome when doing so. Carrick Cottage was just a few miles from the Lough shore, but we went there only occasionally, deterred perhaps by the roughness of the road, which was not tarred and so was heavily pitted with huge potholes, caused by the weather and the milk collection lorries, which made up nearly all the traffic. There were other roads but they did not go to the water's edge, and were equally difficult, so that we did not go down to the Lough as often as we might, although sometimes we crossed it by the bridge near Derrylummomd, which was a popular spot for fishing. It was there that I saw an angler with blood running from his fingers, which had been bitten deeply by a pike, which he had caught and was trying to release from the hook.

As far as I could tell, apart from fishing, Upper Lough Erne was little used by local people; a yacht or dinghy or vessel of any kind was a rare sight, and the only regular users of the lake were some children living at its eastern end, who went to school by boat each day. Things are different today, for at holiday times in particular, both the Lower and Upper Loughs are busy with craft of all kinds, and Fermanagh has become a haven for fishermen and naturalists, who are keen to enjoy its unspoiled countryside. Although busy, the Lough and its banks are never crowded, and it is good to see tourism being developed to make such areas of outstanding natural beauty and interest readily accessible, without creating the problems of excessive use, which are met with in parts of the English Lake District and the Norfolk Broads. There is plenty of scope of course; there is more water in Lough Erne than in the Lake District and the Norfolk Broads put together!

I recall cycling over the red painted metal bridge at Carrybridge, and thinking how utilitarian a structure it was; how was I to know that it would become a well known watersports centre, worthy of advertisement in the national press? It is encouraging to see how Fermanagh has been opened-up, with the improvements in its roads, the development of Forest Parks, and the access for visitors to such places as Florencecourt, which was still a private house when I was at Kinowla. All this has been done without spoiling its essential atmosphere of peace and quietness, and it is of benefit to the local people also, who now use the amenities of their county much more than they did. I would have no trouble finding the Marble Arch now! The sight of a boat in the driveway or yard of a house is common, and the children enjoy the freedom and facilities of Upper Lough Erne, although their parents and grand-parents hardly knew of it at all.

In company with almost all the young people of the district, our main indoor sport was badminton, which both Elizabeth and I had played before, but not with the seriousness, almost fanaticism, shown by some of the local players. Each small community had its hall, usually tiny, and where there was a hall, no matter how small, there was a badminton club, which met once or twice a week, such meetings being most important events for many of the members, who would have played every night of the week if the hall had been available. In remote parts of the countryside were many men who lived alone, and some of these in particular, played badminton with the sole aim of winning, and could not appreciate a less devoted attachment to the game. They found it impossible to enjoy any game which they lost.

It was, of course, their only interest beyond what was, for most of them, the dullness of their everyday lives; it was also their only encounter with competitive sport of any kind, so that a 'win at all costs' aim was understandable, although it was completely at variance with their kindly, easy-going attitude to life in general. The badminton court was the only place where they were 'hard men,' and off it they were gentle and helpful: forgetting this, I was often in trouble when my approach to a lost point in a doubles game failed to match that of my partner! All the players did not share this outlook, and the club evenings and matches, were pleasant social activities, with the matches attracting many spectators and much applause.

After the game there was the inevitable marvellous supper with cakes and buns, sandwiches and sponges (inches deep!), as light as half a feather, and filled to over-flowing with cream. It was incredible to think that all this superb baking had been done at the edge of hearth fires, in three-legged pots, blackened with age and use, and covered with burning peat, and with no other aids at all. No wonder that the girls who could accomplish these culinary miracles were in such great demand as wives, so much so, that at one match, a clergyman complained that badminton matches were the main cause of most of his young lady parishioners leaving his flock.

Almost all the halls were too small for a full size court, but this in no way diminished the enthusiasm with which badminton was played. Lighting was provided by Tilley lamps around the walls, and frequently games had to be held up so that the lamps could be taken down, and pumped up to restore the light to its former brilliance. Matches were played between clubs many miles apart, and I remember travelling a long way to play one game, only to find upon arrival at 9.00. p. m. or so, that no suitable shuttles were available. Someone was despatched post-haste to Cavan, which was 20 miles away, for some new shuttles, and the game eventually commenced less than an hour later, so that obviously no speed limits had been observed, and presumably some unlucky shopkeeper had had a peaceful evening disturbed. Not that he would mind very much, for country shopmen were most obliging, and would think little of finding a breathless figure at the door, at half-past nine at night, saying,

'Could you open up the shop, John, and get me a couple of dozen shuttles quickly now?'

That particular encounter did not end until early next morning, and much later than expected, so that on our return journey, the Customs man at the Border had to be brought from his bed to let us through. He was reluctant to leave home, and the resultant delay meant that it was about four o'clock when, at long last, we reached Kinowla. At school later that morning, I was in a state of great confusion when revising with the class how to work out the area of a triangle; the puzzled

expressions on the faces of the children told me that something was amiss, and I then discovered that I had been talking
about rectangles and not triangles at all. Meanwhile of course,
some of my fellow badminton players were still in bed, for they
had no need to rise early when they did not wish to do so.

I often wondered how badminton had become so popular
in such an isolated area; it was not taught in schools, and is a
relatively sophisticated sport requiring specialised equipment.
It is not easy to play and has a relatively complicated scoring
system, yet it was enjoyed by many people who had never
played any other game. The halls were already there, but
racquets and shuttles had to be bought, and this was difficult,
as few if any, of the players were affluent, and most were unable,
or unwilling to spend money on anything but essentials. This
was a surprising trait of farming folk around Kinowla, for they
were kind and generous with material things like eggs and
potatoes, but reluctant to use money, even though it was
beginning to become more plentiful. No doubt memories
lingered of harder times, when cash was scarce, and these
helped to prevent any thoughtless expenditure, although the
monthly cheque for milk helped to alleviate what we have now
learned to call 'cash flow problems.' Nevertheless equipment
was bought, sometimes I am sure, with many misgivings, and
badminton became a universal game, whilst others such as
tennis, cricket, even football, remained unplayed, indeed
unknown. It helped to pass many a dull winter evening, and to
fill many otherwise almost empty lives.

The local badminton club met in the Orange Hall in
Kinowla, which was also the venue for the many entertainments, which played a prominent part in the social life of the
community. These had many exotic names: Basket Tea, Ameri-
can Tea, Guest Tea, Variety Concert and Soirée among them,
but they all consisted of a supper (despite the 'Tea' of the title)
and various forms of entertaining acts by singers, musicians,
actors, reciters and comedians. Children from the school often
appeared in these items, the proceeds of which were always in
aid of a charity, and Mrs Hopkins was well to the fore in
arranging for her well-connected friends to take part. They
were generous with their time although their talents were
limited. I recall one lady, of more than ample proportions, but

sadly reduced singing skill, who had literally to be pushed up the narrow stairs leading to the stage, which she then dominated, in every sense, with her presence. Another of Mrs Hopkins' aristocratic acquaintances was a popular titled performer, whose act consisted of music hall songs, which he sang with gusto to the wheezy accompaniment of a concertina, played by himself in a manner best described as improvisatory. His favourite number was *I don't work for a living*, which was certainly true, but he was so unassuming and friendly that he remained a much loved figure.

> 'If I can't have sunshine without any work,
> I'd rather stay out in the rain!'

he would sing, to rapturous applause from a smiling audience, most of whom had to work very hard even in the rain, but who ignored the irony, if they saw it at all, and enjoyed the performance.

I was intrigued by all these amusements, especially by the word 'soirée,' which I had never met before, outside of the pages of a book, although the *Oxford Dictionary* states that it was first used in 1820, and means, 'an evening social meeting, with tea etc.' As befitted its French origin and high society connotations, a soirée was generally held to be superior to most other entertainments, although this was not reflected in the quality of the performers, which was never very high, but even in early nineteenth century Bath, the 'tea etc.' cannot have reached the standards of that provided in Kinowla for a soirée, or for any other function, no matter how it was designated, which were always of the very highest. Indeed for many of the guests, the food was the high point of the proceedings, and was worth waiting for, no matter how indifferent the fare provided by the performers.

Yet a few years later, television was to come, bringing with it an entirely new world of entertainment, with a wealth of fresh experiences. It has much to answer for, but I am sure that it has brought colour and excitement to many isolated people, enriching their lives and creating new interests. It is a pity that in so many cases this has been at the expense of the old activities, but in Kinowla, at least some of these are still carried on, not unchanged, but with renewed liveliness and vigour. There has been an upsurge in dramatic activity, songs and music are still performed and concerts continue to be organised, and I hope that in all of this, some of the seeds sown at school have taken root and flourished.

7 Some Neighbours

HE NEVER FAILED. Every time we went away from Carrick Cottage for more than a day or two, within a few minutes of our return we would hear a cheerful voice call loudly, 'Welcome back to rural Ireland!' and going outside, we would see a sprightly, well-built old man, waving a stick in the air and repeating his cry of welcome for all to hear. It was George McBrine, our neighbour from the farm along the road to Derrylummond, who, so his daughter told us, always waited for the bus from Enniskillen to stop at our door when we had been away from home, and would then hurry forth to greet us.

His farm was some distance from our house, and there was a house just across the road from us, with a little group of cottages beyond that, but in all but distance, George was our nearest neighbour, although we were very different in almost every aspect of our lives. All our neighbours were good ones, warm, friendly people, who helped us in so many unsought ways. Whenever we had visitors, shortly after their arrival, someone would be at the door with a jug of milk; we might go away for an afternoon and find some potatoes or vegetables left at the door, and they were always glad to look after Oscar and Yorick for us. Most of all they understood that we were strangers in a strange land, and without making us feel uneasy or patronised, they helped us to adjust to our new life, and to be at home among them. But George went even further than that, and shared with us all his lively good-nature as a true friend.

Despite his meagre schooling at a small country school similar to Kinowla, (which he had left early), he was well-read and of quick intelligence, and given the opportunities which present-day children have, he would have gone far in life. As it was, he had travelled to England and worked in various jobs around Liverpool before coming home again to look after the farm in the townland of Aughafad, where, when we knew him, he was living with his wife Martha, his daughter Vera, and his youngest son Alfie. When we went to cailey with them, George was quick to start a discusion with me upon some topic of the day, sometimes political, since this was the time of the 1945-1950 Labour government, with which he had little sympathy, and sometimes religious, as his fundamentalist views were opposed to my less rigid ideas. There is always some clergyman in the news for his unconventional outlook upon the Bible; of late this has been the Bishop of Durham, and before him, among others, the then Bishop of Woolwich, Dr John Robinson, the author of *Honest to God*. In George's time this place was occupied by the Bishop of Birmingham, who had published some 'advanced' views on religion, which, according to George, were contrary to the teachings of the Bible, which George often read, and knew thoroughly. George had never forgotten or forgiven him for this, and there were times when he appeared to hold me personally responsible for all that the Bishop had said, so that I often found myself having to try to find reasons for the Bishop's views, or what I thought they might be.

Often we would talk about less controversial matters, and George would regale me with a wealth of stories about the countryside. He knew many tall tales, which he tried to convince me were true; an Englishman was a fine target for a joke, especially as he liked to regard me as a kind of city slicker, who knew little about unsophisticated rural life, and would believe anything. Sometimes he was right, but there were others when his leg was pulled just as hard by me, as mine was by him. One story from the many which he told to me, remains in my mind, for it has all the hall-marks of a traditional folk tale, unlike others which were merely 'fairy stories,' as he well knew.

The story was about a family who lived on the shores of Upper Lough Erne, and had a local reputation as herbalists, and as people who knew charms and cures of various kinds for human and animal ailments. One day two of the brothers from that family were crossing the Lough in a boat, on their way to an island, to cut down some trees. Unfortunately on their way back, the axe fell from the boat and disappeared under the water. Later that day, a knock came at the door of their cottage, and when they answered it, they found a little man standing outside, dressed in the green jacket and red cap of the 'wee folk.' By means of signs, the wee man indicated that he wished them to take some medical supplies and go with him. They did so and he signed that they were to take their boat and set out over the lake; acting upon his instructions they rowed across the Lough until, coming to a spot near the island, which they had visited earlier, they were told to stop rowing, and then the boat began to sink slowly beneath the water.

When they reached the bottom of the lake, they found several wee folk surrounding another, who had a deep gash in his head, obviously caused by an axe, which lay nearby, and which the brothers recognised as the one which they had lost. Realising what was required of them, they set to work to treat the wound, bathing and cleaning it, before applying healing herbs and a bandage. The wee folk were delighted, and made signs to the brothers which they found difficult to understand, but which they finally interpreted as a promise that, should the wee man recover from his wound, then the brothers and their family could go out upon the stormy waters of the Lough without fear of accident or upset. Tradition has it that this did happen, and that the brothers and their descendants have never yet had any difficulty on Lough Erne, although they have sailed in conditions when no-one else would venture out; no doubt their attention to the wee man was successful and he must have recovered from his injury.

Writing down the gist of the tale utterly fails to re-capture the quality of George's narration, the changing timbres of his voice, his facial expressions, the merry light gleaming in his eyes and the shadows dancing around the big farm kitchen, cast by the flames of the turf fire, but they are all there in my memory and still shine down the years, as does another incident of a very different kind. Martha, Vera and Elizabeth had gone to a soirée in Kinowla, and I had gone to keep George company, after finishing my work. I was late in arriving and after our usual chat, George set about making some supper for us. He made tea in two big mugs by putting a spoonful of tea into each, and then pouring the water straight on to it; next, using a huge carving knife, he cut some enormous slabs of bread from a half- used loaf.

Using the same knife he proceeded to spread butter on the immense slices of bread, and we then sat down to enjoy it all, amid a scene of utter chaos. The table was littered with crumbs, the loaf lay in one place, the butter, still in its wrapper, in another, and between them was the tea caddy, left wide open and surrounded by spilled tea. Across them all lay the carving knife, thick with butter, but we enjoyed our supper, oblivious to the mess, until the door opened and Mrs McBrine entered. She was horrified and shamed by all that she saw, for she obviously thought that George had let her down by treating the guest with such lack of manners. In no time at all the table was cleared and covered with a cloth, a pot of tea was made, and thinner slices of bread cut from the loaf, to be spread with butter from the butter dish, using the proper knife! The tea was served in china cups and the bread and butter placed on china plates, yet it didn't taste any better than George's less delicate offering. However Martha's dignity as a good housekeeper and hostess had been restored, especially as she ensured that we were given much more than plain bread and butter, and plates laden with cakes and buns appeared from nowhere!

I last saw George McBrine one Monday evening in the early summer of 1949. Elizabeth had gone to cailey with Martha and Vera, and I had arranged to come to meet her just after ten o'clock, as I wanted first to listen to a radio production of 'The Playboy of the Western World.' I had never heard the play before, so that my head was buzzing with its ideas and the magic of its language when I left home to collect Elizabeth. It was a glorious evening, and a red sun was setting behind long drifts of white cloud, when I met Elizabeth and Martha at the end of the long lane which led to the farmhouse. 'Come on up to the house,' said Martha, 'I'll make you some tea' knowing that I never refused such an invitation. On this occasion however I tried to do so. 'No thanks,' I replied, 'it's already very late.' although by Kinowla time it was still early. Martha thought so too for she retorted, 'Not at all, and George will never forgive you if you come this far and don't come up to see him.' There was no answer to that so we all went up to the house and stayed there until midnight. I told George about the play and he was adamant that nowhere in Ireland would people think that a man was to be admired because he had killed his father, with a loy or anything else. When we left, the sky was cloudless and bright moonlight silvered the gentle landscape, which was folded into deep peace and tranquillity.

The following afternoon at school just after lunchtime, I was taking a lesson in geography and had asked the children a question. From several who had raised their hands to reply, I chose Hughie Britton to give me the answer. 'Well Hughie, and what have you to say?' 'Please Mr Claypole,' said Hughie, 'Mummy said to tell you that George McBrine died this morning.' 'What was that, Hughie?' I asked unbelievingly. 'What did you say?' Hughie repeated his message and looked around to the other children for support, for he realised that I was so surprised by the news, that I could hardly take in, or believe, what he had told me. 'Did you say that Mr McBrine is dead? Are you sure that's right?' Hughie nodded, and again sought support from the others, but they knew even less than I did. At last the news made its way into my dazed mind, and for a long time I stood still and stared at the children without seeing them, but I remember that everything went silent, and I was aware of a sudden hush, although there was rarely much noise in the school at any time. Most of the children knew George, if only by name, but only a few would have known of my friendship with him, yet they all sensed that something had happened to cause me much sadness, and I like to think that by their silence, they were showing their sympathy to me. After such a shock I was unable to carry on any more direct teaching, but the class continued to work from their books, in an atmosphere of great seriousnesss and little movement, realising that they should not trouble me any more that afternoon.

I was numbed by the news and by the way in which it had reached me, and passed the rest of the school day with no sense at all of what was happening, hardly looking at the children, and unable to comprehend what I had been told, although I hoped desperately that somehow, Hughie had made a mistake, and that the burly figure of George would still be pottering about the farm, or sitting at the fire, when I went up to Aughafad after school. After all, how could Hughie have known what had happened, when he had been at school all day?

When school finished and all the children had gone, I rushed home, where Elizabeth met me at the gate, and the sadness of her face told me that the news was true. I realised that I had forgotten that the Britton family lived so near the school that they all went home for dinner; Hughie would have been told about George then, and Mrs Britton would have instructed him to tell me. With this realisation came the confirmation which I had been dreading, that George McBrine was dead, and I would talk with him no more.

I came into the house and Elizabeth told me what had happened. After breakfast George had gone out to the byre, where he had had a sudden heart attack and had died almost immediately. Both of us were desolated by all this, and as soon as we could we went along to Aughafad, where a wake was already in progress, but we did not stay long amid the noise and bustle of so many people, in a room where on so many occasions, the only sounds had been the soft Fermanagh voices of George and his family, our happy laughter and the hiss of burning peat upon the hearth. I did not go in to see his body, preferring to remember George as I had known him, lively of face and mind, but I was glad, so very glad that I had finally agreed to go up to see him on the night before he died. Apart from his family, Elizabeth and I were the last people to see George McBrine, and I know that I will never forget him.

The houses down the road from us were all occupied by people called O'Neill, all with the same initials, and three of them with the same Christian name. At the side of the road lived James O'Neill and his wife, behind them was Joe O'Neill, who lived with his son, who was also called Joe, while another Joe O'Neill, old Joe's nephew, lived next door. To add to the confusion they all had the same address, which presented the postman with a difficult problem when a letter came for Mr J. O'Neill, especially as they were all most annoyed if the wrong person opened the letter. In the district the three Joes were all known by nicknames, which made them easily distinguishable; Joe, the old man, was called 'Strider' because of the long steps which he took when walking, his nephew, a keen card player, was known as 'The Dealer,' whilst only his son answered to Joe.

Strider was a lively old man but without the breadth of interests and knowledge which made George McBrine so distinctive, but it was he who claimed to have heard the fairies but had not seen them. He just loved to tell the story to anyone who would listen, and as he did so his face would light up, the years would fall away, and he became lively, as he described how he had heard the clink of metal falling in the road, but had gone some distance before he had realised that he had dropped some coins from his pocket.

'I left the bike in the hedge,' he went on, with the excitement beginning to grow in his voice, 'and went back to pick up the money. All of a sudden I heard little voices and wee silvery laughter, and I knew that the fairies were there.' Strider looked around quickly and began to tip-toe along the road towards the coins, when suddenly he stopped, for his heart was beating wildly, his lips were dry and his scalp tingled. Should he leave the money for the wee folk to use, or should he go on to see the fairies for himself? Perhaps they would see him first and resent being disturbed by a clumsy mortal, and who could tell what might happen to him then? By now his voice had dropped once more, but it started to rise again as he continued, 'Sure didn't my Joe get trapped in a field, and he hadn't even heard the wee folk, let alone seen them!' Then the tones grew stronger and more confident. 'But wouldn't it be a wonderful thing for me to see the fairies for myself?' he said, and his bravery shone through his voice, 'and wouldn't that be a great story for me to tell afterwards?'

Armed with this thought of fame and renown, Strider set off again, as quietly as he could, but when he reached the shining coins, there was no-one there; despite all his precautions the fairies must have heard him and disappeared. He picked up the coins, and, ever the optimist, thought that he would still have a good story to tell, for even if he had not seen the fairies, he had heard them. 'And who in all this country can say that?' he would demand loudly, as if to defy anyone to do so. No-one ever did of course, and Strider went on telling the tale for many years, no doubt adding to it from time to time, but not once did he reveal what he had been doing in Skenbarra, and just what his condition had been, when he was cycling home on that momentous night.

His son Joe was a lively young man, friendly and cheerful, and of an open disposition, which possessed a certain innocence and naivety. Joe often spoke without thinking too deeply, and sometimes these characteristics combined to make him appear an amiable, but somewhat gullible rustic. He often told of his visit, with Mary his wife, to Dublin, when neither of them had ever been any further than Enniskillen; people had treated them so kindly, and they had been given so much attention, that they had been made to feel very important.

As things began to improve on the small farm which he ran for his father, Joe applied for a government grant to improve his byre, and the cottage in which they lived, but was informed that to qualify for aid he would have to install running water in his cowshed, and a bathroom in the house. Joe was indignant. 'Bathroom!' he exclaimed, 'Bathroom! What do I want with frills?' and he agreed to improve the byre but not the cottage. This was a perfectly understandable reaction, for I am sure that he knew no-one who had a bathroom at home, and in any case hadn't he and all his long family been brought up without one, and weren't they all fine people? Now water in the byre was different, for that would make his work easier, and although he was very hard working, he was all for that.

Like George McBrine, Joe liked to tell local stories, and one in particular, which I am told, crops up in traditional tales from other parts of Ireland. It was the story which had perturbed Strider on the night when he had heard the fairies. 'I had been to a dance,' Joe would say, 'and I'd had a wonderful time. All the girls wanted to dance with me, and I did my best to oblige, so that when the dance ended, I was worn out. I jumped on my bike, but was so weary that I could hardly push the pedals round, so I decided to lie down in a field for a nap before I rode on home, as I had a long way to go. It was a bright moonlit night and I could see everything clearly when I climbed over the gate and lay down to sleep just inside it. At last I woke up and went to climb over the gate on to the road again, but, try as I might, there was no gate to be found, and the field was surrounded by a thick hedge.'

Joe went on, 'I couldn't get through that hedge, so I just lay down and went to sleep once more in the moonlit field. In spite of everything I had a good sleep, and when I woke up, it was broad daylight. The sun was shining down, and there, just beside me, was the gate, with my bike lying outside it. So I jumped on and rode home. But I still wonder why I couldn't find the gate the first time!'

Whilst we were living in Carrick Cottage, Joe and Mary suffered the immense sadness of losing a baby, and were in great distress about it, especially as it was their first child. Elizabeth and I went to see them, and were each offered a drink, whiskey for me and port wine for Elizabeth. The drinks had been brought in specially for all the expected visitors since Joe and Mary, like ourselves, were non-drinkers. I would take nothing but orange juice but, with many misgivings, and in order not to embarrass our hosts, Elizabeth accepted the port, which she had never tasted before. She was handed a large glass filled to the top with wine, and she proceeded to gulp it down as quickly as she could, for she didn't like it at all. Nothing was said at the time but some while afterwards Mary was talking about us to Martha McBride. 'Isn't it great,' said Martha, 'that the Master never touches a drop of drink!' Mary smiled. 'Yes,' she replied, 'but his missus can't half knock it back!'

A little while later on, I was coming home from school when I saw a police car parked on the road outside Joe's house, from where two policemen and the local R. U. C. sergeant emerged, with Joe following behind, most reluctantly. They crossed the road, headed along the path up the hill, and we watched the little procession enter a small stone building on the hillside, come out again and return to Joe's cottage. Eventually the policemen drove off carrying a bottle, and we went across to find out what had happened. Joe was spluttering with fury, although he was usually very quiet and calm.

'Did you ever hear tell of the like of it?' he gasped. 'Looking for poteen in my house and a drop of drink never passes my lips!' 'That's terrible,' I agreed, 'but did they find any?' Some of Joe's indignation faded. 'Yes,' he said. 'When we lost the baby, somebody gave me a bottle for the visitors, but there was only a wee drop left; just enough to cover the bottom of the bottle that's all.' 'What will happen now?' I asked. 'They'll take me to court and I'll be fined I suppose. And it's all your fault.' It was my turn to be astounded. 'My fault? What's it got to do with me? I was at school wasn't I? And I don't drink either!' Joe grinned and his face lit up as he forgot his anger. 'Yes, you're to blame, for if you'd had that drink when you came over to see us about losing the baby, there would have been no poteen left, and the police wouldn't have found any today!' He smiled again. 'Anyway,' he went on, 'if they do fine me, I'll get my own back.' He was happy once more, so I didn't query this remark, and thought nothing more about it. At the next Petty Sessions court in Derrylummond, Joe was duly charged with possession of poteen, and was fined £10, but he did not appear perturbed. When I saw him again I commiserated with him, for £10 was a considerable sum then, but he was surprisingly philosophical about it. 'Och! It wasn't too bad,' he said, clapping me on the shoulder and laughing, 'I smuggled some calves last week and got £12 of a subsidy for them, so I'm £2 better off!' He had got his own back, with a vengeance!

These events reminded Elizabeth that before they all happened, one morning she had a severe cold, and after I had left for school, she was going to bed with a hot drink, when Mary O'Neill called at the house. 'What's wrong with you?' asked Mary, and upon being told, advised Elizabeth to take a hot drink and go to bed. 'That's what I'm going to do,' replied Elizabeth, 'I'm making a cup of cocoa now.' 'Cocoa!' laughed Mary, 'That's no good at all. Just you get into bed and I'll bring you something better than cocoa.' She soon returned with a small bottle containing a colourless liquid, half of which she heated and put into a tumbler. 'Drink that now,' said Mary, 'and keep the rest until later.' Elizabeth did as she was told, and was soon fast asleep.

When I arrived home from school, late that afternoon, I found the front door locked which was most unexpected and had to let myself in, only to discover that the fire was out, everything was cold, and Elizabeth was still sound asleep in bed. When eventually she did waken, she felt much better and her cold had gone, so she put the rest of the unknown liquid away in a cupboard, where it had been when the police had passed by our house to search Joe's mountain shelter for poteen. Now we knew what the mysterious 'cold cure' was! We'd had more poteen in our house than Joe had had in his, and he'd been fined £10 for having it! We consoled ourselves by thinking that ours was to be used for medicinal purposes only!

Many months later, when our poteen bottle was empty, its miracle cures having been effected, and there was no possibility of any action, Elizabeth told Sergeant Bingham of Kinowla R. U. C. about what had happened, and he was highly amused. 'If only I'd known,' he laughed, 'what a great catch that would have been. Two finds of poteen in one day! A big haul for us and what a story for the *Impartial Reporter*. . . and the Master too!' Joe O'Neill was equally amused and said that the police would be well advised to keep a sharp look out upon us, to find the source of our supplies!

Like all our neighbours, Joe's schooling had been very limited, but he had great respect for books, which was increased when I was able to tell him about a slipe, which is a kind of wheel-barrow, but without wheels, which is used in the peat bogs for moving turf which has been cut. 'How do you know about slipes?' he demanded. 'You've never been in a turf bog in your life,' which of course was quite true. 'I saw a picture of a slipe in a book,' I told him. Joe exclaimed, 'You can't have! They don't have things like that in books.' He was surprised and fascinated when I showed him *Irish Heritage* by E. Estyn Evans, which is full of information about country life in Ireland, with lots of pictures of farming and turf cutting implements, and he was delighted also to find that he already knew much that other people had to learn from books.

Across the road from Carrick Cottage, where the stream deepened sufficiently for me to fill a bucket with rough water for washing-up, was another white-washed cottage with a thatched roof, which was in poor condition. The walls were no longer white, the woodwork needed painting, and the roof, which had once been well covered with a thick coating of straw, was now a patchwork of the dark ochre of the original thatch, bright yellow splotches where repairs had been carried out, and the green of the grass, which was growing in odd places all over the roof. For weeks on end, especially in winter, I would see no-one at the cottage, and then I would chance upon Paddy Cowan, who lived there, standing at the door, or upon a ladder, stuffing handfuls of fresh straw into a hole in the roof, which had grown so big that it could no longer be ignored.

Once when I commented that I hadn't seen him for a long time, he laughed and said, 'Och! I'm like the hedgehog, and hibernate in the winter,' and I am sure that there was much truth in that remark. Yet Paddy was no simpleton, although he seemed to have little contact with the contemporary world, but I could not understand how he made a living. I cannot recall ever seeing him away from the house, and can only presume that he and his sister, who lived with him, were able to manage with the potatoes from the garden, the eggs from the hens which scratched around the cottage, and the milk from the few cows which they kept.

It was wise though, never to under-estimate the folk living in Kinowla, and this was brought home to me with great force, one evening when I had gone to the stream for water. I found Paddy there, but in a vastly different mood from his usual lethargy and apparent indifference to the world. 'Did you ever hear tell of Robert Louis Stevenson?' he began, and went on to surprise me by discussing *Kidnapped* and the other novels with knowledge and interest. As Stevenson had never been one of my favourite authors, Paddy probably knew more about him than I did, but he confessed that he had not read *The Black Arrow*, and asked if I had the book at home, as he would like to read it. 'No,' I said, 'but I'll get it for you from the library,' and Paddy was pleased when a copy was sent to him from the County Library in Enniskillen. I told him that he could borrow other books from the library, but I do not think that he ever did so, as he seemed content to pass his days doing as little as possible, apparently happy and satisfied with his way of life, and certainly he did not attempt to change it. I hope that he returned *The Black Arrow* to the County Library, and assume that he must have done so, although that would have required a tremendous effort on his part, for I never heard anything from the librarian about it.

High up on the face of the hill behind our house, were three cottages, again occupied by men of the same name, but so isolated from each other as to give rise to no confusion. The highest of the three, situated in an oasis of green fields among the surrounding bog cotton and heather, and commanding a superb view over the countryside below, to the island-studded waters of Upper Lough Erne, belonged to Peter Malone, who lived there with his aged mother. Peter was a tall, quietly spoken man of about 30, he always wore a cap and his face was that of a much older man, wrinkled and weather-beaten from the harshness of life on his upland farm. Although it was so remote, Peter's house was tidy and spotlessly clean; obviously his mother kept a sharp eye, and I suspect, a sharp tongue, upon him, although she was unable to do much about the place herself.

Peter kept his bike in our outhouses so that I saw him often and had many conversations with him, for he was an interesting personality of much intelligence but little formal education. When I spoke to him about his school-days, he said, 'I was hardly ever at school.' 'Why not?' I enquired. 'Did you not go to the school in the village?' for, being a Roman Catholic, he would not have attended Kinowla School although he would have walked past it each day, when he was a boy. 'Not very often,' he replied, 'for every morning I had to load the milk cans on the donkey and bring them down the mountain to the creamery in the village. Then I had to do some shopping, and when I got back again with the donkey, it was too late for school. Then I went to the creamery again in the evening.'

It was a wonder that Peter found any time to go to school at all, for it was a long, steep and stony descent from his mountain home to the road. Tired after that long and difficult walk, the donkey must have walked to the village even more slowly than usual, especially as it had two heavy milk churns slung across its back. The return journey would have been even slower, for although the churns were empty, this time the hill had to be climbed, and the path was rugged even for a donkey. Despite the rarity of his appearances at school, Peter Malone was a knowledgeable man, especially about the sky and the stars, which were spread out before him from his cottage high on the hillside, like a great curtain. He was keenly interested in the 'Northern Lights,' the aurora borealis, which he must have seen often from his lofty perch. He was eager to learn more about them, and whenever I saw a magazine or newspaper article on the subject, I gave it to him, at his request, although it seemed to me that he must know all that there was to be known, as he was so widely read on the Northern Lights and astronomy in general.

However Peter was no starry-eyed dreamer and lived very much in the present. Once I asked him about the fairies, but he laughed and said, 'If there were such things, then I must surely have seen them, for I'm up and down that mountain path at all hours of night and day, and I've never seen or heard anything of them!' But Peter's knowledge of the ways of the world could sometimes be suspect. We were having a cup of tea together, and I gave him a slice of the richest of Elizabeth's rich fruit cakes, which he ate with relish. When Elizabeth came in, Peter was sitting at the table enjoying his third or fourth slice, and he said to her, 'Mrs Claypole, this is very good bread.' Apart from the everyday soda or wheaten bread, his mother probably did little baking for him, for although she must have been a tall, strong woman in her prime, she was now old and slow but by no means frail. If we were walking past the cottage we called to see her, for we were sure of a warm welcome, as she saw few visitors and rarely left the house.

The only time we saw Mrs Malone away from her cottage was on a fine day in July 1948, when Elizabeth discovered her sitting on the low bridge beside our house and enjoying the sunshine. 'Don't sit there,' she said, 'come in and have some tea.' Mrs Malone's reply was polite but firm. 'No thank you, I'd rather stay out here.' 'Are you waiting for Peter?' Elizabeth asked, realising that it was strange to see her so far from home. 'Not at all. I'm waiting for the bus.' 'But it's only one o'clock and the bus doesn't come till three.' 'Sure don't I know that, but I only come down once a year, and I'm going to make the most of it, and see all that's going on.'

It transpired that every July Mrs Malone went to stay with her daughter in Bundoran, and that this was the one time in the year when she left home, so Elizabeth made her some sandwiches and tea, and left her to enjoy the excitement of seeing the half-dozen or so vehicles which would pass before the bus came. It is certain though, that all the drivers and passers-by would stop to talk to her, and that would be thrill and pleasure indeed to Mrs Malone, who probably would speak to more people that afternoon than during the rest of the year, when she was isolated in her lonely cottage on the hill-side.

But that proved to be the last time Mrs Malone waited in such excitement for the bus, because before July came round again, she was dead. She made her final journey down the mountain path, borne upon the stout shoulders of her family and friends, on a dark day of low cloud and drizzling rain. A large number of men had gathered at the foot of the path to await the arrival of the coffin, but the path was muddy and slippery, so that it was a long time before it reached the road and the waiting mourners. It was a melancholy sight to see the bearers emerge from the mist with their heavy burden; the sad cortege came slowly and carefully down to the waiting hearse, which then set off on its way to Kinowla chapel, followed by a long procession of men, who had now ceased their chatter and walked silently and reverently to bid farewell to a much respected lady. The only bright spot of that gloomy day was that despite the bad weather, so many had gathered to pay their last respects to Mrs Malone, and our sorrow was obvious as we walked behind her to the chapel.

Her old home is now ruined and desolate. Without the constant spur of his mother's presence, the difficulties of maintaining such an isolated house and farm proved too much for Peter, who left it and moved away. Eventually he made his way to London, but how he could possibly have lived there I do not know, for how could a man accustomed to the freedom of the mountains, and who knew the stars and the Northern Lights as his friends, ever be content among the traffic and fumes and noise of the rushing metropolis? Now he too is dead, and his body lies beside his mother's in Kinowla.

Peter Malone was very different from his two namesakes who also lived in isolated cottages across the face of the hill from him. One was nicknamed 'Dan's Peter,' and was always as neat and tidy in appearance as was his home; his feeling for order and cleanliness was well known- 'and him without a woman too,' as the wagging tongues said so often. If 'Dan's Peter' was famed for his tidiness then 'Peter Malone the Third,' otherwise 'Clatty Peter,' was notorious for the squalor in which he lived. When he was seen in the village, which wasn't often, his clothes were always ripped and torn, as if he had tried to clamber through a thorny hedge on his way down from the mountain, and rumour had it that he did just that. 'Clatty Peter' was reputed to buy a second-hand suit and then tear it to shreds by walking through bushes, and too close to hedges, just as if his eyes were so bad that he could not see where he was going. Certainly on the few occasions when I spoke to him, he stared into my face from a very short distance away, in a short-sighted manner, and poor vision would account for many of his eccentricities. On his remote farm high up the mountain, he kept some cattle and a flock of hens, and as he never closed the outside door, the hens wandered into the house to roost, and to keep him company among the sacks of meal. Consequently he was alleged to sleep with his head in a barrel, to keep the hens away from his face, and while I had not seen this, I have heard of similar 'clatty' people (clatty meaning dirty, hence the nickname), elsewhere, who did exactly the same for similar reasons, and so I have no reason to doubt the story.

A friend of mine tells of an old lady who lived in county Down many years ago, who every month came to the fair in the nearest town carrying two large buckets of eggs to sell, the empty buckets being used to carry home any groceries which she had bought with the cash from the sale of the eggs. Often she became so drunk at the fair that she was unable to reach her home, so she emptied the buckets and, putting them under a hedge, placed her feet in one, and her head in another, and went to sleep. One night when she was more drunk than usual, she had hardly reached the outskirts of the town before settling down to sleep with the aid of her buckets, and was found by the police. Feeling sorry for her, they took her to the police station, gave her a bed for the night, and breakfast next morning, before sending her on her now sober way. Highly delighted with such luxurious treatment, she took good care to rest near the town after the next fair, and upon being found by the police and receiving the same hospitality, she used similar tactics equally successfully the following month. At last however, the R. U. C. decided that she was becoming too regular a guest, and ignored her when she tried her tricks again. This so upset her, that she stormed the station, hammering at the door and thumping the windows, demanding admission, seeking arrest for creating a disturbance, in a vain attempt to obtain bed and breakfast yet once more. As he had been instructed, the policeman on duty turned a deaf ear to all this, and she was forced to rely upon her buckets for shelter, when she was again too drunk to make her way home from the fair.

Clatty Peter wasn't as artful as that, and lived a grubby, lonely and aimless life with his hens and heifers on the hillside. Yet, despite the discomfort and inconvenience, to say the least, of their conditions, these mountainy men appeared to live happy and contented lives, free from pressures, and in good health, for they never seemed to be ill. They troubled no-one and no-one interfered with them; their possessions were few, but so were their needs, and they never complained. They were not envious either, although I suspect that Peter Malone, the star-gazer, would have liked a bicycle with tyres which did not puncture; a set of new tyres with deep treads would have been sufficient, and better than the bald ones which gave him so much trouble so often in our outhouse. Or did he just want a constant supply of 'good bread'?

Very different from the Malones and the O'Neills was John Britton, who owned Carrick Cottage, and was the connoisseur of spa water! He was quiet and dignified, and his ready smile helped to shield his reluctance to commit himself too quickly when new ideas were being put forward. John was always very helpful and appreciated all that I was trying to do at the school, and this was most valuable, as four of his children were among its pupils.

He lived with his wife, Rachel, in a house which was larger than most in the neighbourhood, as befitted a J. P. of long standing, but nevertheless, Mrs Britton had to work hard to care for the children, look after the home, and carry out the many tasks expected of a farmer's wife, no matter how large her house. With no labour-saving devices to help her, she spent much of her time in the heat of the open hearth fire, baking bread and cakes, boiling meal for the hen's 'meat,' and cooking for her large family; even just keeping the fire going was an endless chore. At the back of the burning turf, Rachel kept a large log, which held the fire together, and burned away slowly; once she surprised us greatly when she announced, 'I'm going out to fetch a stick for the fire,' and returned, dragging a large part of a tree trunk, which, despite the heat, she wedged into position behind the fire.

From then on, 'Mrs Britton's stick' became for us a synonym for anything heavy or bulky, but it also reminded us of the friendly welcome which we, and many others, always received at her house. We were there often, and many times left very late at night; on the afternoon following one extra-late departure,

Elizabeth apologised to Rachel for keeping her up so late. 'Not at all,' was the reply. 'After you left, Willie Smith and Annie came, and stayed till four o'clock!'

The redness of her complexion, a slight stoop of her back, and the slowness of her movements bore eloquent witness to her unremitting toil around the farm and in the kitchen, and the installation of a coal-burning range must have come to her as an immense relief, after her long years as the servant of the hearth fire. This came for Rachel Britton and many other hard-working housewives around Kinowla, in the autumn of 1950, after a more than usually wet late summer, when so much rain fell, that in many fields, grass for hay remained uncut, and turf could not be dried in the bogs; the consequent shortage of peat forced the replacement of many traditional fires. The heavy rain also meant that the level of local rivers was exceptionally high, as I realised to my horror, one Sunday afternoon in September 1950, just before we left Kinowla, when Elizabeth and I allowed ourselves to be taken out on the Claddagh river by Norman Taylor, the father of Pauline, Colin and Charles, to whom we were paying a farewell visit.

Norman and his family lived near the river just before it entered Upper Lough Erne, and he insisted on taking us for a trip on the Lough in his boat. We knew that he was an expert and experienced boatman, but that was small consolation when we saw the condition of the river that dark, blowy, showery afternoon. Normally it was quiet and placid, but then it was in full flood, and had become a torrent of angry, brown water, bearing upon its heaving back, debris of many kinds, including branches of trees and even a dead cow. The wind was so strong that we could hardly hear Norman when, just after he had launched the boat, he called, 'Look out for floating tree trunks! The water's so high that some are being washed down, and they're hard to spot!' I looked apprehensively at the rushing river and then towards the lough, where white horses were being whipped up by the wind; I turned up my coat collar, thrust my hands deeper into my pockets and determined to make the best of it. The afternoon was so dull, and the lough so broad, that we could not make out anything beneath the sky of leaden grey, except the dark, rough water, and the boat's white wake tossing behind us in a long turbulent line, which was soon swallowed up by the surrounding darkness. It was bitterly cold, and to complete our discomfort, the rain started again, its barbed drops stabbing maliciously against our uncovered faces.

Norman chose that inauspicious moment to make his way down from the stern where he seemed very comfortable, and took something from his pockets. 'Here you are,' he said, 'you'll enjoy these,' and gave us each an orange, which out of courtesy, we had to peel and eat, there and then, despite our cold, wet fingers. Oranges are difficult to manage at the best of times, but in a restless small boat, on the waters of Upper Lough Erne, in half a gale, on a rain-sodden afternoon. . . we ate the fruit and thought longingly of the sunshine of their homeland. But that was not all, for hardly had we finished, when Norman came to us again. This time he brought us bars of chocolate, which were easier to handle than the oranges, although what we both wanted was a seat by a warm fire, and a hot drink!

Those delights were a long way off, as Norman was determined that we should have a full tour of the Lough before we left Kinowla, so we cruised steadily on to its eastern end, where we turned back, only to head into the full force of the fierce westerly wind. If we had been chastised with whips before, we were now chastised with the scorpions of raindrops as sharp as needles, driven hard into us by the high and relentless wind, but we were consoled by the thought that we were on our way home.

That consolation was short-lived, as to complete our misery, the engine spluttered, gave one or two coughs and stopped. Now what was going to happen? Unlike ourselves, Norman was utterly calm, or appeared to be so, just as we struggled to be. He came down the boat once more, told us not to worry because all that had happened was that we had run out of petrol, went back to the stern and searched for the petrol can. After what seemed an age he found it, and we watched with trepidation as he filled the tank and tried to re-start the engine. Would it start again? We hoped fervently that it would, for the boat was wandering aimlessly in the waves, and bucking like a broncho at the Calgary Stampede. The first time Norman tried, nothing happened; the next time he pulled the cord, the engine gave a hiccup or two but nothing else; the result of the third attempt was a purr, which lasted for ten seconds before the engine was silent again; but at the fourth pull, a full-throated roar covered even the noise of the wind. Norman gave a little smile and we set off once more.

He had planned to take us the whole length of the Lough, but darkness was beginning to fall, and when we reached the mouth of the Claddagh river, we turned along it and headed for home. In the gloom we recalled Norman's warning about floating trees, but he was in complete control, and at last we reached his mooring, and then the warmth and comfort of his home, where Mrs Taylor had tea ready for us. 'Did you enjoy your sail?' she asked, and I hardly knew how to reply. 'Well it was an adventure. But I must say that I wasn't very happy when the engine stopped.' Norman said, 'I told you not to worry, it's always happening, and I'm used to it.' 'That's all very well,' I retorted, 'but what about when the engine wouldn't start?' Norman laughed. 'Oh! that! That was nothing. It always takes four pulls to make it start again.' I didn't reply, but picked up my knife and fork and began to eat my tea. It was delicious, but even more important, it was piping hot!

8 Colleagues and Friends

I HAD BEEN at Kinowla for some time before I met any teachers other than Mrs Hopkins, and that seems odd to me now, for I have since learned that we are a gregarious profession, anxious to meet our colleagues, and to discuss the shortcomings of our employers and our pupils. Anyone listening to a group of teachers, especially in a school staffroom, talking about their charges, must fear for the future, for apparently none of the children has much talent or ability, and all of them give nothing but trouble and behave badly. I think that there is a masochistic streak in teachers, which makes us dwell on our problems and difficulties, whilst our successes are mentioned only rarely. I fell into a trap of this nature when I attended my first meeting of the local branch of the Ulster Teachers' Union, and came home very upset because the only topics which aroused any attention were salaries and pensions, at the mere mention of which, heads jerked, tongues were loosened and flagging interest revived. With experience I realised that in the enthusiasm of youth, I was misjudging my colleagues, for I found them to be keen to talk about education, and ways to improve their teaching, at the drop of a blackboard duster, and the Union gave much time to educational matters; indeed I have often complained since, that teachers talk about nothing but teaching! At that first meeting, however, the movement of the heads of the mainly elderly members present was clearly visible, when superannuation topics were raised.

Probably it was because most of the teachers in the area were so much older than I was, that I had so little contact with them. In 1948 young teachers were still scarce, as the output of the training colleges had been greatly restricted because of the War. This meant that isolated places like Kinowla had trouble

97

in finding new teachers, and as staff left, they were replaced by temporary teachers, often untrained, or by retired teachers pressed back into service. When the War ended, and training colleges returned to normal, the number of student teachers increased dramatically, and the opening of Larkfield Training College which was near Belfast, specifically for students newly released from the Forces, of whom I was one, also helped to ensure that by 1948 more teachers were becoming available. As jobs were plentiful, few of these wished to go to remote rural schools, and as far as I could tell, I was the first newly qualified teacher to come to the Kinowla area for many years, and from a professional point of view, I felt most lonely.

As soon as I heard that a new teacher had been appointed to Teelin Public Elementary School, I cycled the six miles to see him there. He was Graham Stevenson, and although we were very different in character and outlook, we became good friends and colleagues, doing much to help each other, if only by acting as sounding boards for our respective frustrations. Graham was a bluff, forthright Ulsterman, born in Fermanagh and immensely loyal to its landscape and traditions, so much so, that having left it and travelled extensively during his service with the army, he had no desire to do so again, and never did. He was happy and contented to be living once more among the hills and loughs of the county which he loved so dearly.

Although like me, Graham was keen to extend the horizons of his pupils, he was equally anxious to further their knowledge of local history and culture, and it is terrible that this man, so steeped in truly national traditions, should have been killed in 1974 by the I. R. A., who would claim to want to advance such knowledge. Graham had deep roots in his native county, together with a wide understanding and appreciation of Irish history and customs; did the gunmen know of that side of his character when they killed him in so cowardly a fashion?

My memories of Graham Stevenson are shadowed by his death, but they remain bright, for he and his wife, Madge, were our first friends in Fermanagh, who had no connection with Kinowla, and it was always a pleasure to visit them at Teelin, where their home was part of the school building. On one occasion they were having repairs done in their bedroom, and temporarily were sleeping in a downstairs room; one morning they overslept, and woke to find the faces of the schoolchildren pressed against the window of their room, which overlooked the playground!

I first heard the Uillean pipes played at Teelin, and recall the piper's elbow waving rhythmically up and down to provide air for the tune which he was playing on his plaintive sounding instrument. This was during a concert in which Graham, Elizabeth and I performed in a sketch which we had written about school life, with Graham as a Billy Bunter-like schoolboy, Elizabeth, a schoolgirl with her hair in plaits, and I, a typical English schoolmaster, of the Will Hay variety, quite unable to control a recalcitrant Ulster class. Asked why she was late for school, Elizabeth replied, 'Please sir, my elastic broke,' and in those non-permissive days, this cheeky retort brought down the house, as did Graham, when he proceeded to eat what he said was a piece of turf, which he had brought for his lunch. The gullible Englishman professed to believe him, as did most of the audience, who were unaware that Graham was eating a piece of gingerbread made specially to resemble a lump of dry peat! What added to the laughter was that teachers were prepared to make fun of themselves, and the children and their parents all loved it, especially when the sketch ended with the teacher being showered with cold water by his pupils. It was far from being Shakespeare, but that sketch is remembered to this day, for only a short while ago, I was given a graphic account of it, by a man who was present at that concert when he was a small boy! He quoted the 'elastic' lines verbatim!

Michael McMillan would have wished to have been in that class, for he had an impish sense of humour and did not stand on his dignity, but when that entertainment took place, he had only just assumed the post of Principal Teacher at Lisnagar School, which was also about six miles from Kinowla, but in the opposite direction to Teelin. We met him after we had called to welcome him to Fermanagh, and as he was not at home, his wife Phyllis had asked us to tea shortly afterwards. When we arrived he was not in, but very soon, a head, surrounded by a duffle coat hood, appeared round the door, and as Michael entered the room, we were aware of lively brown eyes and a big moustache, as a bubbling voice said, 'Hello Elizabeth! Hello

Jack!' as if we had known each other well, instead of being total strangers.

This was typical of Michael's warm, friendly nature, and he bustled around in his mercurial way, delighted to welcome us to his home, making it plain that he and Phyllis were pleased that we had come. He was short and dark, with hair to match his long, black moustache, but his darting eyes revealed his quicksilver character, usually ebullient and happy, but subject to sudden changes of mood, when he became morose, in a manner which was quite alien to his normally cheerful outlook. Michael had great skills as an artist, and an artistic temperament to accompany them, which made him a man for the big gesture and the sudden decision; he was flamboyant in action and dress, and he brought gaiety and colour with him wherever he went.

In those days clothing was still rationed and it was difficult to obtain a new suit, not only because clothes were scarce, but because they were also expensive. Michael found this irksome, as he liked to dress smartly and well, so that he felt great joy when at long last he was able to buy a new suit, his first for many years. He was so proud that he made a special journey to Carrick Cottage to show it to us. It was most unfortunate then, that in an accidental collision, a pot of tea was spilled all over Michael's prized suit, much to his distress. However the stains were removed and he was soon his familiar self again, with brown eyes twinkling and his moustache shaking with laughter.

Michael, Graham and another mutual friend Johnny Turner volunteered to take part in a concert which I had arranged in aid of the school, with some friends from Belfast as the 'stars.' Elizabeth, the schoolchildren and I were also in the supporting cast. On the afternoon of the show, a final rehearsal was held, and then Graham, Michael and Johnny went to Skenbarra, ostensibly to do some shopping for Madge. They did not arrive back until we had tired of waiting for them and had commenced the entertainment, but when they did reach the hall, what they had been doing in Skenbarra was soon clear, which was more than could be said for their heads! However, only Michael was not in control of himself, and as the evening proceeded he grew more and more incoherent, to the astonishment and glee of the audience, but to my dismay and embarrassment, as we had no idea of what would come next from him. We struggled through to the end in a welter of missed lines, unrehearsed actions and impromptu remarks, some of them decidely risque, but bringing the loudest laughs of the evening! The audience may have been happy but I was not. As soon as the concert was over, Michael went straight home to bed, still wearing the black burnt cork make-up which he had plastered on for the final minstrel show. Fortunately for him, Phyllis was away in Belfast, for he would have received an extremely warm welcome from her, but had she been at home, Michael would not have gone to Skenbarra anyway!

The following day we travelled to Belfast with our friends and Michael and his dog. It was a strained journey in a small van, with hardly a word spoken, and even the dog must have felt the atmosphere for he was sick and had to be allowed out to recover. Afterwards when we all returned to Kinowla, little was said about what had happened, but the temporary aberration in our friendship soon passed without recrimination. Life was too short for that, and in the remote world in which we lived, friendships with people of all kinds were essential, especially with colleagues who shared the same interests, faced similar problems and provided zest and stimulation to the routine matters of everyday living. Such stimulation was vital, for without it, life in Kinowla could easily have become so enclosed, that we would have been isolated from all our previous activities, and cut off from the life of the busy world outside. Had it not been for our friends, and for the radio, which was our life-line to the world beyond the Fermanagh countryside, it would have been possible to forget other spheres of existence, even during the period of the post-War Labour government, which brought so many changes and created such a ferment of discussion and social experiment. All that we knew of this around Kinowla was the large number of people who found themselves, most of them quite rightly, in sudden need of dentures and spectacles, now that they could be obtained free of charge, and the repeated complaint of a local clergyman, that he had to pay nine shillings and a penny each week for a National Insurance stamp for a man whom he employed; inevitably he was nicknamed 'Nine and a penny!' Hence we

were glad of visitors to Carrick Cottage, and it was not long
before they started to come. Only a few weeks after our arrival,
Elizabeth happened to be at the school when the door opened
to reveal, to the consternation of the children, who were not
accustomed to unexpected visitors, a friend of ours from
Belfast who had driven the 40 miles from Omagh to see the
strange surroundings in which we were rumoured to have
settled. He had managed to find us, in spite of the directions
which he had been given on the way, and which had led him
to doubt our wisdom in living among such odd people, for he
had been unable to find our house. The school was better
known, and easier to track down. He overcame his bewilderment very quickly, and was soon one of our most frequent callers.

Many people came to see us, after travelling long distances
by the standards of those days, but this was not a tribute to our
popularity, but more because we lived close to the border with
the Irish Republic, where petrol, butter, sugar and other
desirable commodities were available freely, whilst they were
still rationed in Northern Ireland, which was only slowly
recovering from the war-time shortages. Many of our visitors
would come with the petrol tanks of their cars almost empty;
they would then drive over the border to Skenbarra, fill the
tanks, then return to Carrick Cottage and syphon off most of
the petrol into tins, before going back to fill up again. When
they went home, they would have a tank filled with petrol, and
several gallons in tins in the boot, to say nothing of a few
pounds of butter and sugar as well.

Not all of them cut things as fine as Billy Gregg, who had so
little fuel in the tank of his car, when he came to see us one day,
that it ran out in Derrylummond. He pushed the car to the
nearby garage, and asked the startled attendant for half a
gallon of petrol, knowing that this would be enough to take
him to Skenbarra and all the petrol he wanted, whilst keeping
as many as possible of his precious ration coupons for use at
home. Billy was prepared to take risks in order to do this, and
on another occasion when he was on his way to Skenbarra to
fill his tank, he ran out of petrol again, but was in luck once
more, for he was at the end of the lane which led to Mrs
Hopkins' house. When we went there to explain our predicament, Mrs Hopkins and her husband, Walter, insisted upon

giving Billy, not only a couple of gallons of petrol, but coupons to buy several gallons more. To round matters off, we were given tea and cakes as well! I had to try hard to prevent Billy from running out of fuel at the same spot on many subsequent visits, but he had lost his skill in 'drying up' at convenient places, and so was never able to enjoy their hospitality again!

Billy was among a group of our friends, who had hired a large but elderly, car to visit us one week-end in summer, during the only spell of really hot weather I can recall at Kinowla. On Saturday morning they all left to go shopping in Ballycolmaine, using the untarred and rough unapproved road, and leaving me to enjoy the sunshine at home. When they reached our door upon their return, I could only stand and laugh at them, as they were covered from head to foot in fine, white dust, and resembled a group of workers from a flour mill where the machinery had gone wrong. All the ridges in their skin were lined with dust, the wrinkles in their foreheads, the joints of their fingers, the edges of their noses and their hair, all were thickly encrusted, and when they moved, white clouds billowed up around their shoes; literally they could hardly be seen for dust.

With the limited resources of water available, cleaning up so many people was not easy, but when at last the dust had settled, an explanation was forthcoming. As it was such a hot day, they had set out with the windows of the car wide open, which was fine on the tarred road, but when they drove along the unmade road, they were assailed by vast waves of dust blowing through the open windows, from the loose surface, which was dry and powdery after a long spell without rain. It was better, they thought to be roasted than choked, but even that alternative torture was denied them, for the car was so old that its body-work had many cracks, crevices and holes through which the dust penetrated insidiously, even with the windows closed, as the over-laden vehicle bumped its way slowly over the rough and stony unapproved highway, unapproved in more senses than one! Almost all the way to Ballycolmaine and back, about twenty miles or so, they had been surrounded by dust; small wonder then, that their appearance had become as 'ghastly white' as the ghost of Tom Pearce's old mare, making its haunting way home from Widdecombe Fair.

All this was forgotten that afternoon, when after a tour of Lower Lough Erne, we rested in a field where the hay had been cut, and collected in the old way into small rounded heaps, which were dotted about like mounds of gold. Against their bright yellow, the after-grass gleamed green, with an intensity only noticed in such contrasts; the hedgerows were decked with sweet scented honeysuckle, and entwined with stitchwort, and bright with campion; the sky was clear blue and the distant waters of the lough shimmered and glistened in the sunshine. A mesh of haze surrounded the landscape locking in the perfumed air, and from afar, a cuckoo called, its cry softened by distance so that it did not cut across the softness of the scene, but merged gently into it, hardly disturbing the quietness and peace of it all. It was the magic of Fermanagh, sometimes harsh, sometimes gentle but rarely as rich and as prodigal with scents and sounds and sights as on that splendid summer afternoon.

Such sensuous delights were uncommon, but pleasures of a lesser splendour were encountered more frequently, and not only in summer. Elizabeth's parents liked to come to us in early autumn when the hills glowed with bracken and brilliant red berries jewelled the shapely leaves of the rowan trees. When the autumn sun shone, it slanted across the land, mellowing the hedges and the fields , and bringing with it something of the lushness of high summer. They came in other seasons too, and Elizabeth's mother liked to busy herself in our garden, often early in the morning. The farmers on their way with animals to Derrylummond fair, would be surprised to find her working so early, and would greet her with respect and friendship. She did not approve fully of our living conditions, but accepted them as our choice, and was pleased that we were living in the country, where she could enjoy herself, as she had when she was a girl in County Antrim.

Elizabeth's father liked the country life also, and nothing pleased him more than to walk the two miles to Derrylummond on the fair day, to wander around in the fair, and to listen to the sounds of the dealers and the animals which they were trying to sell. He liked the old traditions of the countryside, and the fair must have reminded him of the many similar events he had seen during his boyhood days in rural County Antrim, where now most of the fairs had died out in their old form, although they had lingered on in County Fermanagh. Derrylummond fair, small as it was, still remained as it had been for many years, with carts and animals lining the street, the air filled with the cries of buyers and sellers, the slap of hands on a bargain, the shouts of hucksters and traders of many kinds, the lowing of cattle, the squealing of pigs, the neighing of horses, and even then, the braying of donkeys. It was all very different from the normal somnolence of the main street of Derrylummond. Yet times were changing even in Fermanagh; an auction mart for cattle had opened recently in Enniskillen, and this was to spell the end of Derrylummond fair and many others like it.

During one of his trips to the fair, Elizabeth's father was enjoying himself watching two farmers bargaining over a donkey; as was the custom the price had been set far too high and, as expected, the reductions were inevitable, but small and slow in coming. In situations like this a third party was on hand to help the dealing, and to bounce the haggling along, in the hope of a reward from the seller when the sale was completed. That day George McBrine was assisting with the transaction, amid much shouting and gesticulation, and attempts to clap hands together to seal the bargain. It must have been a great sight, for George was a character with a ready wit, and Elizabeth's father was standing on the edge of the crowd, puffing his pipe and quietly enjoying the banter, when suddenly George looked across at the onlookers. He was holding aloft the right hands of the two farmers, trying to persuade them to conclude the sale, but when he spotted Elizabeth's father, he dropped them instantly, and forgetting both farmers and the donkey, came over to him with the familiar greeting 'Welcome to rural Ireland,' and shook him warmly by the hand. They wandered around the fair together, and finished up with a quiet drink in one of the village pubs before walking back home.

A drink of a different kind was endured, if not enjoyed, by Elizabeth's brother Stephen, who after a long time at work, and some intensive study and examinations at Queen's University, Belfast, came to stay with us for two weeks of rest and recuperation. Certainly he needed it, for when we saw him getting off the bus with his younger brother Richard, we were appalled at how run down he looked; his eyes blinked continually and he sniffed and coughed frequently, a nervous and unnecessary cough, which was very disturbing. Later that evening Elizabeth commented to me about this. 'Stephen looks terrible,' she said, 'and we'll have to do something to improve him before he goes home. I'll go to the chemist tomorrow to see what he can recommend.'

Richard and I went for a walk up the hill path, but Stephen was too tired to come with us, and Elizabeth stayed at home with him. It was such a lovely evening that we walked on and on, and when we reached home again it was late and almost dark, but we were surprised to find no-one about, and the house in darkness. Even more surprising was the smell which pervaded the house; I didn't know what it was and found it unpleasant after the sweet scent of the evening air along the path. Elizabeth was fast asleep, and I was unable to find out what had happened until breakfast time next morning, long before the two boys came down.

'What were you doing while we were out last night? There was a terrible smell in the house when Richard and I came in. What was it?' I asked.

'Don't you know? It was poteen of course.'

'Poteen? Where did you get poteen last night?'

'You've a very poor memory. We had some in the cupboard in the kitchen. It was all that was left of the poteen which Mary O'Neill gave me, when I had that very bad cold.'

Then I remembered that there had been some of the colourless liquid left in a bottle, and that I had wanted to throw it out, but Elizabeth had refused, saying that it might come in useful if she had a cold again. I was mystified about what she had done with it. 'Surely you didn't take it?' I went on. 'You haven't got a cold now have you?'

Elizabeth smiled, a pitying smile. 'Not at all,' she said, 'but I gave some to Stephen to see if it would help him, and then I sent him off to bed early.'

'What good will that do?' I retorted. 'Poteen won't cure his blinking and that cough!'

'You never know. After all it cured my cold didn't it?'

In the face of that logic I gave up and reasoned that there wasn't much poteen anyway, and surely so little could do no harm. When Stephen appeared for breakfast that morning, he was a changed man. His blink had gone, there was no more coughing, and the little sniff which had accompanied the cough had vanished also. 'I'm hungry,' he said. 'What is there to eat?' Elizabeth was overjoyed that her poteen cure had worked so quickly, but she hadn't finished yet. 'You can have all you want,' she told him, 'but first you must take this.' She went into the kitchen and came back with a raw egg, which she cracked into a tumbler. 'All right,' agreed Stephen, and he swallowed the egg in one gulp before proceeding to eat a huge fry of eggs, soda bread, bacon and tomatoes. 'That was good,' he said, when he had finished, and was sprawled in our most comfortable chair, 'I'll have that every morning.' and so he did, with the addition of a pint of milk, warm and fresh from one of Joe O'Neill's cows, which he had helped to milk.

As was his custom when we had visitors, Joe came to cailey and he and Stephen got on well together. Stephen was interested in farming and was keen to do some milking so Joe needed little persuasion to allow him to help, not only with the milking but with the general work around the farm. Stephen enjoyed this enormously, especially as Joe was a tolerant taskmaster, and there were many opportunities for conversation, which suited them both. Every morning Stephen went across to Joe's byre and did some milking, after which he drank as much new milk as he wanted, before coming back for his raw egg and his fry, and then going out to the farm with Joe.

One day they were working together in the fields when an aeroplane flew over, which was rare enough, but this one came down low over the farm and they could clearly see the pilot. Joe stopped work, as he did at the slightest provocation, removed his cap as he looked up, and turned to Stephen in shocked disbelief. 'Would you look at that now!' he exclaimed. 'Would that be one of your friends from the university do you think?' He scratched his head before replacing his cap. 'How did he know you were here? You must be very well known, up there in Belfast!' With a shake of the head, Joe resumed his haymaking but Stephen went on watching the plane until it vanished from sight, then he too picked up his rake and began to work again, wondering if Joe was having a joke at his expense. . . or was he serious? He has never able to make up his mind about that!

After two weeks of such treatment, but no more poteen, for

the bottle was now empty, Stephen returned home, rested and renewed, and freed from all symptoms of illness; no wonder that his mother hardly knew him, but neither did she know of the vital role which poteen had played in his recovery, for she would not have approved of that! But some friends, hearing about the raw eggs, have muttered that the cure was worse than the disease.

Of all our visitors at Carrick Cottage, none had travelled farther than Elizabeth's Uncle Willie and Aunt Effie, who lived in a tiny outpost called Sioux Look Out, which is near the shore of Lake Superior in Canada. Their home was even more remote than ours, with its name conjuring up visions of vast open spaces, unpeopled and empty save for wandering bands of Indians, and on the very frontier of the white man's advance across North America. They were most interested to come to Kinowla, which they did from Belfast in a tiny Austin 7 driven by another of Elizabeth's uncles, and they did not consider that we were isolated at all. 'Why, you've got a town only 12 miles away,' they said, and never before had Enniskillen assumed the mantle of some great metropolis, for that is how they made it appear!

During their stay, we all squeezed into the little car and set off for Sligo, about 50 miles away, which was far enough in such cramped conditions. We were glad to stop overlooking Glencar Lake for some lunch, but there was consternation, mostly from me, when we found that we had forgotten to bring a kettle to boil water for tea. Uncle Willie was not put out and said that he would go to the nearest cottage to borrow a kettle, oblivious of the fact that in that hilly countryside, there was no sign of a house. Nevertheless, after a long wait, he returned in triumph with a kettle blackened by age and soot, explaining that the cottage was far distant and was not too clean or tidy. After our lunch the kettle was cleaned and taken back to its owner, who by then, had changed her dress, put on a fresh apron and tidied the house. This amused Uncle Willie, who did not think the cottage at all remote, but I'm sure that in, what was for us, a lonely spot, the lady saw few unexpected visitors, and one from Canada would be very exotic, and worthy of special treatment.

We proceeded to Sligo, and to our surprise, found that the town was crowded, for on that day, the body of the poet W. B.

Yeats was to be buried in Drumcliff churchyard, in the area where he had spent a vital part of his life. He had died in France in 1939 but because of the War, only now, nine years later, could he be interred, as he had wished, in his own countryside. As he had written:

> *Under bare Ben Bulben's head*
> *In Drumcliff churchyard Yeats is laid.*

Despite the solemnity of the occasion, the atmosphere in the town was like that of the annual races, with everything cheap and tawdry, even the smudged paper emblems, bearing a crude likeness of the poet, which were being sold like raffle tickets, by numerous boys and girls. There was no indication of the ultimate destination of the money which was being collected, and I could not work out how the sale of such gimcrack emblems was connected with the homecoming of a great poet. Few of the throng in the crowded streets seemed to know or to care about who Yeats was; the idea was to make as much money as possible from the event, and there was no sign of respect or reverence for a great man; the rejoicing was quite out of keeping with such a serious day. When we reached Drumcliff with its round tower, we found Yeats' new resting place near the church, and read his own enigmatic epitaph:

> *Cast a cold eye*
> *On life, on death.*
> *Horseman pass by.*

That seemed an ironic comment on the milling crowds in the streets of the town, only a few miles away.

Upon our return home we were dismayed to find that we had not taken the key with us and so were locked out; I was upset at this for I wanted to hear the broadcast of Beethoven's Choral Symphony, which then was played on the penultimate night of the Henry Wood promenade concerts in London, and it was almost time for it to begin. I brightened up when we found that a small window had been left open at the back of the house, but the only one of us who could possibly squeeze through it was Elizabeth, who consequently had the honour thrust upon her. The four of us lifted her level with the window, which she opened to its fullest extent, and was able to push her head and shoulders through it; then with much wriggling from her, and encouragement from us, she squeezed further until her arms were through also, and she could rest her hands on the table, which was below the window. Still holding Elizabeth out horizontally, we pushed her again until she was lying on the table and safely through into the house.

We were in time for the concert, and after such an eventful day, the thrilling sound of Beethoven's triumphant setting of Schiller's 'Ode to Joy,' ranged widely through my mind long after the choir had ceased to sing, and the orchestra to play. Since then the music of Beethoven's Ninth Symphony continues to evoke memories of Fermanagh, although the music's grandeur is far from the peace of the Lough Erne countryside. Yet there is a quality of truth and satisfaction about them both, which fills the memory with contentment, although the powerful sound of the music cannot have been very faithfully reproduced by that battery–powered radio set, with its tiny speaker. However that set was sufficient to keep me in touch with music, for which I was completely dependent. There were few if any concerts in Enniskillen at that time, and even if there had been, I could not have gone to them, as the last bus for Kinowla left at 6.15. p.m., although on Thursdays and Saturdays, it did not leave until 9.15. p.m., to allow late night revellers to have their final fling! As a life without music is incomprehensible to me, the value of that little blue box cannot be over-estimated, which is why it has such an important part in these recollections.

We paid many visits to Sligo, for it was one of our favourite tours, passing the Marble Arch to Lough McNean, then between the twin villages of Belcoo and Blacklion, and on across a desolate landscape to Manorhamilton. The road then followed a deep valley among lonely hills, reaching open country beyond Glencar, and stretching through green fields to Sligo town. At the eastern end of the beautiful valley of Glencar, the road forked to skirt Glencar Lough; the southern, and major (relatively!) route kept to a shelf high above the lake, and we often stopped there to admire the view across the lapping waters to the mountains beyond. The minor road to the north however, passed the Glencar waterfalls and then hugged the edge of the lough for a mile or two, until both roads joined again, in flat fertile country.

It was on this northern road that we had stopped to picnic

on the lough shore with some friends from Belfast, who had again hired a large car, to come to stay with us. The road was narrow, and in our attempts to park the car as near as possible to the verge, we succeeded only in running its near-side wheel into a deep sheugh along the roadside, and we could not push it out, no matter how hard we tried. Now what was to be done? The road was little used and there wasn't a house or building of any kind in sight, but we were making another attempt to free the car, when along the road came a man on a bicycle, the first 'traffic' we had seen since our arrival.

When he saw us he stopped and came over to the car. 'What's wrong?' he asked. We explained our predicament and went on, 'Is there a house near here where we could ring a garage?' 'Just a moment,' he answered, 'I'll see what I can do first.'

He was a big man, but we were all astonished by what he proceeded to do. Going across to the rear of the car, he planted his feet firmly on the road, put his hands under the bumper, gave a heave upwards, and another to his right, and there was the large car with all four wheels on the solid asphalt again. 'There you are', he said. 'You'll be all right now.' and he jumped on his bike and pedalled away. We were so amazed by this feat of strength that we were still looking at one another in wonder and relief, when we realised that our Good Samaritan had gone, but we ran after him to express our thanks and appreciation.

He was dismissive of what he had done. 'Och! It was nothing,' and he waved his hand in an airy gesture. 'Now I'll be getting on to my work.' and once more he rode off in the direction of Sligo, apparently unaware of how helpful he had been to us. We had not escaped unscathed though, for a tyre had punctured, and whilst we were changing the wheel, several other men cycled past, obviously on their way to work, although we could not understand where, for Sligo, the most likely place, was six miles away. When we went on our way again, we solved the mystery, for a mile along the road, was a quarry, where the shift was just changing, so the men must have been quarry workers, which would account for the strength which had been used for our benefit. Yet I marvel at it still-one, two, three, lift!. . . one, two, three, heave!. . . and there was the car on the road again; raised by a man who had arrived out of nowhere!

In view of the importance attached to them by contemporary educational thought, I should also have been surprised by the lack of formal parent-teacher relationships at Kinowla, but must confess that I was not concerned that such contacts did not exist, and cannot recall any parent making an appointment to see me about the progress of any child at the school; neither was there any specified occasion when parents could come to the school to discuss their children's work with the teachers. Instead, anyone who wished to do so would stop me on the road, or talk to me after church, or in the village, or come to visit me at home, but few did even this. One parent who did so was Tommy Hamilton, the father of Nellie and Walter Hamilton, who called to discuss with me Nellie's chances of passing the Qualifying examination. The principal of one of Ulster's then most prestigious preparatory schools once remarked that it was easier to pass the Oxbridge entrance examination than it was to pass the 'Qualifying,' and although grossly exaggerated, this view will confirm that Nellie's chances were slim, for whilst she was a pleasant and hard working girl, her intellectual endowments were about average, and far from the standard required to 'qualify' for a grammar school place at that time.

Tommy and his family lived at the distant end of the next parish, far from the school and the village, and when he called at Carrick Cottage one evening, I had not met him before. I did not know who he was and neither did he tell me, throughout the long conversation which we had. I thought that he was some unknown neighbour coming to cailey, so we chatted about the weather and the crops, the price of cattle, the high cost of animal foodstuffs, and the merits of farming and teaching, but only gradually did it occur to me that he had come to see me about something connected with the school. However, he did not tell me what it was, and the supply of farming topics was fast running out. Nowadays I would ask his name immediately and apologise for not knowing it, but then I was inexperienced, and in any case, such directness would have been regarded as bad manners. In the country, it was thought correct to talk around a topic, drawing nearer and nearer to it until finally converging upon the real point at issue. I had no reason to know who he was but Tommy would have been upset if I had confessed my ignorance, and so I had to begin a slow process of discovery, without being too direct, or making my lack of knowledge obvious to him, although Elizabeth had guessed what was happening, and was amused by my dilemma. She went out to make tea, and looked in at me through a small window behind Tommy's head, finding it difficult to keep her face straight, and so making things even more difficult for me.

At last came the vital clue which I had been seeking for so long. Tommy said, 'All this rain makes life hard for people like us.' I nodded sagely, as if I knew exactly what he meant. 'That's true, but we'd complain if we didn't have enough.' 'Aye, but if there's no rain, at least the river doesn't rise so much, and the kitchen isn't flooded. We're never done fighting to keep the river out of the house.'

This was the opening which I wanted, for only two of the families at the school lived near enough to the river to be flooded that often; the Taylors were one and the Hamiltons the other, and as I knew Norman Taylor, this must be Tommy Hamilton! 'Yes, Mr Hamilton,' I said with some bravado, 'it can't be very pleasant for Mrs Hamilton and you when that happens. And it makes it hard for Nellie and Walter to get to school if the road is flooded, doesn't it?'

Elizabeth came in with the tea, having given herself time to restore her composure, and she nearly dropped the tray when she heard me mentioning names with such abandon. Tommy took his tea and sat there eating his cake; now that I had provided him with an opening, he was quick to use it. 'I'm sorry about that Master, but it can't be helped. How are they getting on at school?' Now we were away, the formalities had been observed and we could discuss the real purpose of Tommy's visit; he was disappointed with my assessment of Nellie's chances in the examination, but accepted it with a good grace. He knew that Walter's abilities were very limited, and compared with him, Nellie shone brightly, but as he saw, hardly brightly enough for a grammar school place. Two hours after his arrival Tommy left, after a friendly chat which had helped both of us; an interview during a formal parents' evening would have been more direct but less informative, and much less memorable.

Another parent who, although only in passing, sought information about his children was Eddie Harvey, when he came to the house with some vegetables. 'How's Lily getting on, Master?' he enquired, more I think because he felt that he ought to ask, rather than to find out, as we met often and he was aware of his daughters' progress. Lily was a plump girl of reasonable ability, but very untidy in her work, and we talked about her for a little while. Then Eddie asked, 'And what about Hazel?' Hazel was seven, a blue eyed blonde with long plaits, who already knew how to use her good looks to their best advantage. Her work was not up to Lily's standard, but she was neat, tidy and attractive. I was at a loss for something new to say about her. 'Hazel,' I said, and laughed, to give me time to collect my thoughts. 'She thinks that her face is her fortune!'

Her father was convulsed with laughter. 'That's a good one. I must tell her mother that!' And so he did, and half the countryside as well, for he seemed not only amused, but proud of my impromptu comment. He left the house still chuckling, and Hazel continued to charm her way through school; we had many visitors to Carrick Cottage and I hope that they all left us as well satisfied as Eddie Harvey that day. Hazel grew into a pretty young woman, she became a hair-dresser and soon married; Lily helps to look after handicapped people, but Nellie did not pass the 'Qualifying' and went to work in a hospital, so that there was a happy outcome to both parental visits.

9 Children Growing Up

FROM A SCHOOL photograph taken on a dark day in February 1948, the children of Kinowla School gaze out at me, the infants sitting on a form at the front, looking cold and uncomfortable, in spite of their brave smiles, and the older boys and girls tiered behind them, in the manner so beloved of all school photographers. The back row must have been standing on another form, for some of them are taller than I am, as I stand there with my pocket full of pens, and my wide trouser legs flapping in the wind. Mrs Hopkins is not in the picture, as, for some reason known only to her, she resolutely refused to take part, which is a pity for I have no pictorial record of her, and I would like to have a photograph of the entire school. Each child is dressed differently, for the influence of the chain-store and the mail-order catalogue had not reached Kinowla then; none of them is well clad for a winter's day, yet they convey an overall impression of happiness, which overcomes Graham Marshall's scowl and Pauline Taylor's defiant glare.

Attendance was good that day for there are 35 children in the picture; perhaps the knowledge that the photographer was coming was responsible for this, although no-one is wearing Sunday best clothes for the occasion, and I notice that, unusually for him, William Martin is absent. More than 42 years on, I can remember them all, but I cannot arrange them into classes as many teachers do with former pupils, saying, 'Jack Daly? He was in Class 5 with Jimmy Barker and Mary Foster.' I recall all the children whom I have taught as individuals, and not as members of groups, but many former colleagues, blessed with a better memory than mine, can do both.

James Boyce is prominent (I'm sure that he came because of the photographer, as this was well before his goal-keeping

115

triumph!) as he is the biggest of the boys, and for once is among his contemporaries and not with the younger children, with whom he spent most of his time at school. Next to him stands John Regan, looking out quizzically from the middle of the back row, knowing that in a few months time, at the age of 14, he would be leaving school to help on his father's farm. It was John, who had pointed out to me, very politely, that one did not 'dig' turf, as I had written on the blackboard, but 'cut' it, and it was John's father who had supplied us with our first load of turf for our fire.

John was a sturdy boy, of a steady and straightforward disposition, unlike his younger brother, George, whose impish grin bears out his lively personality, and lights up the whole picture. George was the live wire of the school, but he could, when it suited him, assume an angelic demeanour, foreign to his true nature. He was rarely absent from school, so that I was surprised when he was away for two days, and upon his return I asked him about it.

'Why were you away from school, George?'

'Please sir, I was at a conference.'

The idea of this little gnome of a boy, with his round, rosy face and mischievous eyes attending a conference, seemed incredible to me, especially in view of his non-academic background. 'A conference, George? What was it about?' I enquired.

'Love, sir.'

My incredulity grew apace. What on earth was a small boy like George doing at a conference about love? Doing my best to hide my amazement, and fearful about what his answer would be, I asked him, 'What kind of love, George?' 'Please sir, the love of God,' said George, looking at me with his eyes wide open, and smiling broadly. That reply was not one which I had been expecting, so I went on, 'Who was running this conference, George?' 'Please sir, the Methodist Church,' he declared, and stood there meekly, a picture of such innocence and virtue, that was worthy of a halo - a Methodist one of course, if there are such things.

I cannot recall the children at Kinowla ever behaving badly, although once, when Mrs Hopkins was absent, one of the infants bit another in a fit of temper at playtime, and I felt compelled to punish him; this was so rare an event that it is remembered to this day. (The culprit went on to play rugby for Ulster!) If anyone did give trouble it would be George Regan, but even he would get up to only minor mischief, caused by his carefree nature, and not committed with any bad intent. One afternoon he must have been more troublesome than usual, for I sent him out of the room, intending to bring him in again after a short while. However I forgot all about him, and had not brought him in when school closed for the day, and most of the children had gone home, except for some boys who had stayed to play football.

It was late March, the hedges and trees were still bare, and as I ran up and down the field with the boys, I had an uneasy feeling that we were being watched, so during a lull in the game, I walked over to the nearest gap in the hedge, and there on the other side, peering through the hawthorn branches, was George's round red face, shining like the setting sun. Realising that he had been spotted, he stood up. 'Why haven't you gone home?' I enquired. 'I want to play football,' he replied. 'Then why aren't you playing with us?' I asked. He hesitated a while and then said, 'Please sir, you told me to go out of the room.' My face must have become as red as his, for I had completely forgotten all about that. 'So I did, but why didn't you join in after school with the rest of the boys?' 'Well. . . I didn't think that you would let me. Can I come and play now?' 'Of course.' I told him, and before I could say anything more, he had jumped over the hedge, taken off his jacket and asked, 'Whose side am I on?' as he ran on to the field and prepared to play.

One of the most endearing qualities of the Kinowla children was that they took nothing for granted; they had so little that they were grateful for anything which they received, unlike some children today, who seem to expect to be supplied with everything, and seemingly have little gratitude for the many things with which they are provided at school. Although these are essential for a full modern education, they include much that we never dreamed of having at Kinowla, where bare necessities were hard to come by, there were no luxuries at all, and even chalk was scarce. I am glad that schools are now so relatively well equipped, and know that still more is needed because allowances have never been sufficient, but I do wish that more appreciation was shown by the fortunate pupils, and indeed by some teachers. Modern children have many excellent characteristics, and most of them are generous and friendly, but few are aware of just how much they are given and how much is done for them; I must add though, that when I have told them about Kinowla and its lack of facilities and equipment, and shown them pictures of the school, they have been shocked and sympathetic, and wondered how children like themselves could ever have attended such a poorly provided and clearly, uncomfortable school.

In later years, and at other schools, whenever I opened a well stocked sports cupboard, with its store of footballs, hoops, small balls and other apparatus for games and physical education, always my mind went back to our first football at Kinowla, which was bought for us by two of my college friends, who had visited us during my first year there, and had been appalled by our many needs. Never having had one before, the children were delighted to have real leather 18 panel football to play with, and they took great care of it. Never has a football received such treatment; it was cleaned and dried after each game, and was kept well inflated, so that it retained its newness for a long time.

I told the children that my friends had given them the football and they remembered David and George coming to the school, for they had arrived unexpectedly, and on a motor-bike, bursting into the room wearing boots, great-coats, helmets and goggles, and resembling creatures from another planet. The class was startled by these sudden apparitions, and watched wide-eyed as my friends took off their motor- cycle clothing to reveal normally clad human beings underneath. They spent the rest of the afternoon at the school and came back next day, talking to the boys and girls, helping them with their work and generally making friends with them, much to their surprise, for I'm sure that never before had there been two extra adults in that room, working with the children and interested in all that they were doing.

Shortly after this, a strangely shy George Regan sidled up to me one morning, as I stood at the front of the class after I had called the roll. He pushed something into my hand, saying as he did so, 'This is to help to pay for the football.' I looked down and saw that he had given me an envelope containing some money and a piece of card, cut roughly to a rectangular shape, with white exercise paper stuck over one side. The card was folded down the middle, and on the outside was written in George's best penmanship:

KINOWLA P. E. SCHOOL
Collecting Card For Football
PRESIDENT: RONALD J. CLAYPOLE
COLLECTOR: GEORGE REGAN

Inside the card on the lined exercise paper was a list of children who had subscribed, with George's name, like Abou Ben Adhem's, leading all the rest; as was evident from an alteration on the card, he had even increased his donation when later on, others had given as much as he had originally. I was immensely moved, and my heart went out to those children who, having so little, had given so much to pay for the precious football, which had been given to them as a present. Although I explained this to them, and offered to return the money, they would have none of it, so we decided to buy another football, and when, in due course it arrived, they might have been endowed with the contents of Aladdin's cave, so excited and pleased were they. When with great pride, I showed the card to some of the parents, they were most upset, not at the collection, but at the 'effrontery' of George Regan, in 'daring' to use my Christian name at the front of the card. 'What a bold boy he is!' they exclaimed with indignation, but I have that card yet, and it is one of my most treasured possessions.

George was a clever boy, who passed the Qualifying Examination and went to Portora Royal School in Enniskillen. I understand that unfortunately, later on he did not choose his friends wisely, and his enterprising and adventurous nature was mis-directed, leading him into trouble with the police. He spent some time in prison and not long after his release, he died. Shortly afterwards his brother John died also; the world is a poorer place without them.

Little did I think when we lived there, that the peaceful district of Kinowla, where nothing of importance to the outside world ever happened, would one day feature in the national news, but it has now done so on several occasions, and all for the worst of reasons, connected with the present 'Troubles.' It has become a difficult area in which to live in peace, but I am glad that, as far as I am aware, no other Kinowla children have been in such trouble with the police, although tragedy has struck some of their homes.

Kinowla was, and still is, such a closed community, that the advent of a new family was very unusual, and if they came from outside Northern Ireland, then that was still more strange. Therefore when the Harper family came from Birmingham to live near Teelin Bridge on the road to Enniskillen, they aroused much interest, bordering on curiosity. It was a big change for them, but they quickly settled down, as did their six year old son Jonathan, who was received by the children at the school as a being from another world. They soon made friends, none more so than George Regan, who lived near Jonathan and took him under his wing. Jonathan's English voice sounded odd among so many soft Fermanagh accents, but he soon became a linguistic sponge, absorbing each voice which he heard, so that his speech altered to match that of his playmates at the time.

One evening Jonathan came into his home when I was there, and when I heard him speaking before he came into the room where I was, I was sure that it was George's voice which I had heard, and so I was surprised when Jonathan entered and there was no sign of George. They had been playing together before Jonathan had come home, and like a vocal chameleon, but quite unwittingly, Jonathan had assumed the cadences of George's speech. Later on I noticed that he did this with other children also, and I wonder if he does the same with the civil servants with whom he now works in England?

When George Regan passed the Qualifying Examination, Hughie Britton was also successful, and there was much excitement in the Britton home when the vital letter arrived. Jim Brown, their farm worker, was given the task of looking out for me as I cycled past the house on my way to school, and he began to wave his arms and to shout, as soon as I came in sight down the road. I was still a long way from him, and I wondered what all the fuss was about. He waved his arms to their fullest extent in a series of wild gestures, as if making himself so big that I would be unable to pass him. 'Master! Master!' he yelled, flailing his arms so violently that I thought they might drop off.

'There's great news,Master, great news!' 'What is it Jim?' I asked, as I jumped from my bike, and wondered what could possibly have caused such a normally undemonstrative individual to have become so excited.

'I'm not to tell you, Master, but come inside and hear all about it,' he continued to shout, although by now I was standing at his side, and was no longer away down the road. Jim was certainly pleased about whatever it was, and called into the house, 'The Master's here! The Master's here!' which was the signal for Hughie to dash out, waving a piece of paper in his hand, and crying, 'I've passed! I've passed!' Then, quivering with excitement, he gave the paper to me. It was a letter stating that Hugh Britton had passed the Qualifying Examination and could go to a grammar school in September; news which was received by all the Britton family, in the same way as the good news must have been received at Aix, when it was brought from Ghent! It was touching to see that Jim Brown's excitement and pleasure matched that of his employer's family, and he too was delighted that Hughie had done so well. We had to wait until the next morning to hear about George's result, as he had left home before the postman called, and we had no telephone in the school. Neither had anyone else, so immediate communication was difficult, although I suspect that John Britton would have found some way of letting me know in similar circumstances! I suspect too, that the rejoicing in the Regan household would have been equally fervent, if more subdued, but perhaps I thought so only because I knew the Brittons better.

Four of the Britton children were at school, where they were quiet but unfailingly bright and cheerful. Under the guidance of her mother, the oldest, Beatrice, was a capable girl about the house, and carried out many domestic tasks efficiently and without fuss. Her movements were quick and birdlike, and she was always smiling quietly, perhaps to hide her shyness. Among the boys, her counterpart was Mark, steady and reliable, and able to carry out many practical tasks thoroughly and well, which was much more important than remembering that 'cubbert' is not the correct spelling of 'cupboard!' Mark was the leading spirit in the little family concerts, which the children put on for their visitors, and he took on a fresh personality when he perched an old trilby on his head, wrapped a scarf around his neck and took up a pipe, at which he puffed contentedly, as he recited a rhyme, part of which summed up the the philosophy of many of the Kinowla folk.

'Whether the weather be bad,
Whether the weather be good,
We'll weather the weather
Whatever the weather. '

Just as Beatrice followed in her mother's footsteps, and now looks after a home of her own, so too Mark took after his father, and he and his youngest brother, Edward, who did not come to Kinowla School during my time there, have run the family farm since the death of their father. After achieving academic success, Hugh and Willie left home and Hugh joined the R.U.C. , in which he was a high ranking officer, before being killed by the I. R. A. Willie went to Trinity College, Dublin, and is now the headmaster of a large grammar school, after a time as deputy head of a grammar school in Belfast, where, he has told me, many of the pupils were of the first generation at such a school, just as he and other 'qualifiers' from Kinowla had been at Portora or Enniskillen Collegiate School.

Whilst it is encouraging to hear of boys and girls making successful careers, it is also good to know that others, perhaps less gifted academically, have made happy homes for themselves and their families, living contented lives as good citizens and neighbours. I am pleased to think that almost all the children in that dark photograph appear to have found a useful role to play in society, at various levels, no doubt, but all adding their portion to the well being of the community. The Taylor family illustrate this as aptly as the Brittons, for Pauline overcame her untidiness sufficiently to become, I am told, a beauty consultant, and I'm sure that her cheerful exuberance would brighten, and make happy, any situation in which she found herself. Her older brother Colin, has been promoted from the position of headmaster of the new Kinowla Primary School to become headmaster of a much larger primary school in County Londonderry. The youngest of the children was Charles and he has gained a measure of fame as an impresario of popular music, acting as agent and manager for various pop groups, and well known in that field in Northern Ireland. I do not think that his time at Kinowla was of any value to him in this career except in a very general sense, and my memories of him are strictly non-musical. In the picture Charles is smiling broadly, and I recall that he usually showed much confidence, certainly at football, when with boots flying, he was always in the thick of any melée which took place, and these occurred often, in games of our standard, irrespective of the position of the ball, which could easily be many yards away from the whirling feet! It was Charles however, who gave me my most acutely embarrassing experience at Kinowla, luckily not long before I left it, and one which still makes my toes curl today; indeed they are bunched up at this moment.

After tea with the Taylors on the occasion of the trip on Lough Erne, I chanced to remark that I was fond of fish, whereupon Norman raised his eyebrows and said, 'But you haven't always liked fish, have you?' 'Oh yes!' I responded, 'I've liked it since I was a boy. In fact, there's nothing I like better.' Norman shifted himself in his chair, smiled slightly, and went on, 'I'm surprised to hear that.' I was puzzled and said so, and I felt put out a little, for how could Norman, who hardly knew me, know so much about my tastes? Sensing my feelings, he looked straight at me, and said, 'Can you remember telling our Charles to take a parcel from your table at school?' I cast my memory back and realised that I had done so, but other children as well as Charles Taylor had been asked to remove things which they had left on my desk. 'Yes,' I replied after a slight pause, 'because I had told all the class not to leave things on my table without telling me, as it was getting so cluttered up, yet next morning the desk was as untidy as ever, so I told them to take the things away, and give them to me later. The children were continually leaving things there and I had to do something about it.'

'I suppose so.' consented Norman grudgingly, and I felt that he knew all about it, perhaps more than I did, for it was only a tiny incident, which had made very little impression on me. 'Did you know that Charles had left a parcel there for you?' I shook my head and he went on, 'He didn't bring it back to you either, did he?' 'I really can't remember, but I don't think so. It can't have been all that important,' I replied. Suddenly I became aware that all the family were listening, and the only sound in the room was the ticking of the clock, and the bubbling of water boiling in the pot above the fire.

Norman's voice became more brisk. 'Charles thought it was important, didn't you?' he said, turning to Charles, who nodded his head vigorously but said nothing. I felt trapped, and remained silent until Norman asked, 'Do you know what was in that parcel?' 'No, I don't, but then, how could I? Well, what was in it?' I asked. 'Two trout, one for you and one for Mrs Claypole,' was the reply. I was mystified. 'Trout?' I queried. 'Who sent me trout?' 'Charles did. He had caught them the night before and brought them specially for you, but when you told him to take the parcel away, he was too upset to bring them back to you, so he brought them home again... and I had them for my tea!'

Although the room was poorly lit, it shone with the brightness of my embarrassment, and the glow of my burning face. I didn't know what to say or do, and after a long pause, I could only stammer, 'Oh! Charles, I'm so sorry. I just didn't know. Why didn't you tell me?' No answer came, and I didn't expect one, but the shadow of my shame hovered over me for the rest of the evening, although the Taylors treated the matter as a huge joke, and were not at all offended. Maybe they were almost pleased at the Master's mistake, and subsequent fall from grace, but I was decidedly uncomfortable. However, the incident taught me, early in my teaching career, of the dangers inherent in blanket decisions, so my discomfort was not without value, though even as I write, I feel warm, much warmer than I did a short while ago, and my shoes seem to be tighter than they were!

The minor road, which eventually reached the Taylor's home near the river, left the main road from Derrylummond to Enniskillen just beyond Teelin Bridge, where Wilfred Carr kept a general store, which, although it was far from any village, was a busy one, serving a number of isolated houses and farms. It was also the stop for buses which did not go to Kinowla village, and that gave it some importance as a junction, but the chief reason for its prosperity was the great variety of goods which Wilfred sold there, from pens to peanuts, to say nothing of groceries and green-groceries, garden tools and farm implements. Nearby was the Teelin Bridge Post Office, the only one known to me which ran out of stamps! It was Christmas time of course, and stamps were in great demand, but it was strange for a post office to have no stamps, and inconvenient too, for anyone who had cycled a long way to buy them.

Wilfred Carr's younger children, Peter and Ella, came to Kinowla School as their older brother and sister, Robert and Margaret, had done, before leaving to attend grammar schools in Enniskillen as fee-paying pupils. Their family was more prosperous than most in the district, but this made little difference to them, and the children were popular at school, although they showed signs of a more affluent background than their friends; Peter even acquired a cricket bat of his own, when cricket was unknown at Kinowla, but I suspect that this was because Robert played the game at Portora. Some years later I heard that Robert had gone to Edinburgh to train as a vet, but as he was not well known to me, I gave this only a passing thought until ten years later still, when the School Nurse came to the school in England where I was then headmaster. 'I've brought you a visitor, Mr Claypole,' she said, and introduced a student health visitor from Alaska, who had come to England for training. As she came to the school once a week we became friendly, and one day I asked her about Alaska.

She told me that she lived in a flat in a small Alaskan town, with a girl from Ireland named Margaret Carr, at which my ears pricked up, for I had not lived in Northern Ireland for 12 years without adopting some of the Ulster habit of seeking friends and relations everywhere, and I asked her where in Ireland her flatmate came from. She replied, 'I'm not sure, but I think that it's Fermanagh. Is that right? Do you know where it is?' My ears were raised even higher. I took a wild guess and said to her, 'Yes, I do. She has a brother who's a vet, hasn't she?' Her eyes opened wide in amazement. 'Yes she has.' she said. 'His name is Robert, isn't it?' I went on. The amazement on her face grew. 'How on earth did you know that?' Now I was sure of my ground, so I continued with confidence, 'She has another brother named Peter, and a younger sister, Ella. Has she ever told you about them?' 'Why, yes. But how do you know about Margaret's family?' she asked. 'Because they all came to the little school in County Fermanagh, Northern Ireland, where I used to teach. I taught Peter myself!' I told her.

She was flabbergasted and so was I, to think that across so many miles, a remote town in Alaska had been connected to a

tiny village in County Fermanagh, and to an industrial town in
the North of England! I have often wondered about Margaret
Carr's reaction when, at the end of her course, her friend
returned to Alaska, with the story, and I hope that it conjured
up many happy memories for her.

Margaret Carr was nursing in Alaska and some other girls
from Kinowla also became nurses, including Helen Kennedy,
who had brought Oscar to us as a pup. Helen was a sensible,
capable girl and I was pleased to hear of her from a teacher
friend of mine, who had the misfortune to become seriously ill
during a visit to Enniskillen. He remained in the local hospital
for many weeks, and became well known to the hospital staff,
and being a teacher, he asked them about their schooldays. Bill
was surprised to hear from one girl that she had been taught
by me; it was Helen Kennedy and I'm sure that she told him
about Oscar and his escapades in Kinowla.

During my college course, I had done my final teaching
practice in Bill's two-teacher school, which was only 10 miles
from Belfast, but far from a major road and extremely difficult
to reach. During my three weeks there I had to go to see Brian
Davey about Kinowla, and so I was absent from the school when
an inspector turned up to see me at work. He had had a long
and difficult journey, and had found the school only after
much effort, so that, after all his trouble, he could hardly have
been pleased to find that I was not there to be 'inspected.' Bill
told me afterwards, that despite his frustration, the inspector
had been philosophical about it, and returned to Belfast at
once, much to my friend's relief, as he thought that he might
have decided to inspect the school whilst he was there. When
I returned to college, I pointed out that I had informed the
staff about my absence, and assured them that I had chosen to
do my final teaching practice at Bill's school because he was
willing to have me, and it was not far from where I lived, and not
because it was almost impossible to find. What is more, they
believed me, and as I heard nothing more from him, I suppose
that the inspector did so as well; perhaps he was glad to have a
peaceful afternoon in the country!

Helen Kennedy smiles gently at me from the old photograph, and there is a white ribbon in her hair, possibly because
she knew that the picture was to be taken, although her older

sister Joan, is just her usual neat and tidy self. Between them stands Florence Martin, looking rather severe, and not doing justice to her friendly open manner, which her brother William also possessed, along with his red hair. William continued to attend school after reaching the school-leaving age, because he was ambitious and wished to keep in touch with education. His father was dead so William could not often be spared from the farm, but for a while, he would come back to Kinowla whenever possible. To make doubly sure, he came to Carrick Cottage once a week throughout the winter evenings, and I would work with him to keep his mind active and alert.

Later he cycled the twelve miles to Enniskillen twice a week to attend classes at the Technical College there, and has since obtained a degree in law. William has had a most distinguished career, which has fulfilled the high potential which he showed during his early days at Kinowla. Yet had it not been for his ambition and determination, he would have been denied this opportunity, and his well-deserved success makes me wonder how many other children, of similar ability and strength of character, have been unable to receive education and training worthy of their talents. That is much less likely to happen now, for even if children do not pass the 11+ examination, equally good facilities are available to many of them them at High Schools, and for those who wish to study away from the atmosphere of school, there are openings in further and adult education, which did not exist for most of the Kinowla children in that 1948 photograph, and still less for their predecessors. In some schools there are difficulties, many of them of a non-educational nature, to be overcome, but in Fermanagh there are many opportunities for those who wish to take advantage of them. From the standpoint of educational opportunity, the old days were not the good ones, but by 1950 improvements were already being made. Although the children in the photograph shared the same school premises, and the same lack of equipment as their parents and grandparents, they looked out upon an educational landscape, which although it was still hard and bleak, was much less barren than it had been of old, and they were being provided with the tools to cultivate it.

Sadly however, for some of those children life was to be too short for such promise to be fulfilled, and James Boyce was not the only one to die young. Almost hidden in the second row of the picture is David Reed, so reticent that he seems afraid of the camera; he made little progress at school and his writing was so poor, that we shared a private joke about it, and said that he wrote 'Reed-ese,' his own language, which only he could understand. David was a cheerful boy, always willing and helpful, and proof that academic ability is not essential for a child to be an asset to a school, as Kinowla would have been a poorer place without his unfailingly bright and bustling presence. It was a great shock therefore, to hear that whilst he was still quite young, David had been killed in a road accident, on his way to visit a relative, who lived in a townland, the name of which David could never spell when he was at school. Neither could I, until I looked it up on a map, and even then, different maps gave different versions. The problem has now been resolved, for at a cross-roads in Derrylummond, there is a signpost bearing the definitive spelling, but too late to help poor David, whom I recall with warmth and affection.

Missing from the photograph, as he had not begun to attend the school when it was taken, was Harry Carson. Because of an attack of poliomyelitis, which had left him with a leg in an iron frame, he was unable to come to school until some years later than he should have done. I have never known anyone so eager to start school as Harry was, and every time I met him, he would ply me with questions about the things we were doing, and would tell me of all that he would do when he was able to come. In spite of the heavy iron on his leg, he was desperately keen to take part in games, even if playing football was beyond him. When eventually he did come to Kinowla, it was with immense joy that he threw balls about, and took part in team games with the others. His academic progress was rapid, although probably this gave him less pleasure than being able to keep up physically with his class-mates, but unfortunately Harry's arrival at the 'Master's End' came just before I left the school, and I was unable to share in his future achievements. He passed the Qualifying Examination and went to Portora, before going on to Queen's University, only to die of a brain tumour, with all his potential unrealised. Memories of the passing of Harry, David, James and the Regan brothers cast a black shadow across the already darkened surface of the old photograph, until I recall them as I knew them as lively and active boys at Kinowla School, whereupon the shadow lifts, the children smile, and all is bright again.

I have written of some of the children who were at that school with me, but there are others whom I have not mentioned, not because they are forgotten, but because they had no outstanding characteristics for recording in a book such as this. Yet they are no less memorable than those whom I have described, and whether as nurses, policemen, farm workers, shop assistants, housewives or factory workers, they live useful lives and contribute much to the common good. In the words of the Book of Ecclesiasticus, (from the Apocrypha), Chapter 38, 'They shall not be sought for in public counsel, nor sit high in the congregation; they shall not sit on the judge's seat, nor understand the sentence of judgement;.....and they shall not be found where parables are spoken. But they will maintain the state of the world, and all their desire is in the work of their craft.'

10   Visitors To School

AT THE END of many school days at Kinowla I performed a conjuring trick which, for a while delighted and startled the new arrivals at the 'Master's End,' and never failed to evoke squeals of frightened pleasure from Hazel Harvey, whose eyes would glisten, as her blonde pigtails bobbed to and fro in excitement. The cause of the commotion was a tiny field mouse which, each day, climbed into the pocket of my coat which hung from a nail at the side of the cupboard, in search of a nibble or two from a sandwich left over from my lunch, which I kept there to take home for Oscar. When I put my hand into the pocket, hey presto! exactly on cue, just like the trained assistant of a circus magician, the little creature would jump out, to the amazement of the ring of spectators, and scuttle across the floor to safety. Once it nibbled a hole in the cap which I had left in the pocket, so deciding that the mouse had outstayed its welcome, I removed the cap and the left-over sandwich from my coat, and from then on, kept them in my mouse-proof bag, so bringing the daily exhibition of magic to a close.

This friendly mouse was the only frequent visitor to our school from the outside world, and on most days our work continued uninterrupted from roll-call to home-time. We welcomed visitors, as I was sure that it was good for the children to see fresh faces and meet new people, but my welcome might have been muted for a visitor who came armed with a bullock, as I understood Brian Davey to tell me during my first days at Kinowla. He was talking about some of the parents, and told me of Harry Allen, who some while ago had been displeased with the then Principal.

'Harry was so angry that he came to the school and brought a bullock with him!' said Brian. I was mystified and could not think how a bullock would assist rational discussion with the teacher, if that was Harry's intention; perhaps if all else failed, Harry proposed to set the animal to chase the principal around the field, but how would he get him out there in the first place? If our college training had not told us how to deal with 13 year-olds who could not read, or how to stoke a fire, still less had it included instruction in the Wild West techniques of roping and throwing steers, and in any case even James Boyce would have been unable to find a lasso in the school, although he had found an axe. With these thoughts passing rapidly through my mind I ventured mildly, 'What did the Principal do about that?' 'He did the only thing he could do. He locked the door and waited for Harry to go away,' was the reply. This cast a new light on parent-teacher relationships. 'Did he have to wait very long?' I asked.

Apparently Brian had not heard my question for he went on, 'And what did the bold Harry do then? He ran around the school bawling and shouting, and every time he came to a window, he stopped and waved the bullock at the Master, and told him, in no uncertain terms, exactly what his fate would be if he didn't open the door. It must have been a really wonderful sight!' It must indeed, for the strongest and toughest of the cowboy heroes of my boyhood did not go around waving bullocks in the air, even very small ones, and this feat was beyond the powers of any of the local people whom I had met. Harry Allen and his family had left the district, and so I did not know them, but I could not think that he would be a rival to Desperate Dan in a display of strength, which would have been unbelievable even in the pages of the 'Beano'; and Desperate Dan was the only character of whom I could think, who would be capable of swinging a bullock around. Yet Brian was a clergyman and surely he would not invent a story like this, except perhaps to fool me! I could do nothing but accept the tale at its face value.

'How on earth did he do that?' I enquired innocently. 'Do what?' he asked. 'Wave a bullock at the Master,' I replied. Brian stared at me in disbelief and then roared with laughter. 'Not a bullock at all! A billhook man, a billhook!' and he made sweeping gestures with his right arm, like a man cutting down long grass. 'Why would he bring a bullock to school?'

I never heard what happened to Harry Allen or to the teacher, but probably all was settled amicably for I was not shown any bloodstains on the floor. Fortunately I had no such angry encounters at Kinowla, although for a while I watched apprehensively if I saw a farmer driving cattle along the road outside the school, and waited until he had passed the entrance, before giving teaching my undivided attention once more!

Perhaps I should have seated one of the boys near a window to keep an eye open for passers-by along the road, as I am told had been the custom of some headteachers of rural schools in days gone by. This was done in the days of little traffic, usually to give the teacher some notice of the coming of an inspector, many of whom were so tyrannical in their ways that they became figures of fear to staff and pupils, and their unheralded visits, sources of worry and dread. Many stories are told of their rudeness and lack of understanding: a friend of mine told me that an inspector's report on his school many years ago, stated 'Many of the children in this school know nothing; the others know next to nothing.' The relationship between inspectors and teachers seems to have been that of master and servant, and not of colleagues seeking to achieve the best education possible for the children of the school. They cannot all have been so dictatorial and domineering, yet enough of them appear to have adopted this arrogant attitude, to cause some teachers to resort to various subterfuges to defeat them, especially when the teachers' salary depended upon the results obtained at the annual inspection.

Inspectors set great store upon what was termed 'oral response,' which usually meant the number of childrem willing to answer a question, and at Elizabeth's primary school, the pupils were instructed that when, in the presence of an inspector, their teacher was taking a class, they must all put up their hands when he asked a question, whether they knew the answer or not. Those who did know were to keep their hands open, but those who did not were to clench their fists; the teacher would then request a reply only from those children whose hands were open, but even so, he was unable to ensure that the ensuing answer would be correct! Nevertheless, with each child in the class wanting to answer every question, the inspector must have been impressed with the high standard of the 'oral response,' which must have ensured a favourable mention in the subsequent written report on the school.

The teaching of arithmetic has traditionally received considerable attention in primary schools in Ulster and I suspect that, whilst much of this is due to the intrinsic value of the subject, perhaps some of it is because many arithmetical questions can easily be set and solved during an inspector's visit to a school, thus giving a quantified result of 'pass' or 'fail,' and so simplifying the assessment of salaries, in the distant days of payment by results. I have often wondered if this might also be the reason for the large amount of rote learning common in many schools in the fairly recent past, when children learned to recite the names of towns in various counties of Ireland, the names of the woollen towns in Yorkshire and cotton towns in Lancashire, rivers and their tributaries, even the names of capes and bays around the coast of Ireland, and strings of many other facts, useful and otherwise. During my training, I was in a school in Belfast when the teacher announced to her class of nine year-olds, 'Homework tonight is all the capes and bays from Malin Head to Galway Bay.' I had no idea of what she meant until my Ulster-born colleagues enlightened me, and even yet I cannot see any value in the exercise, except to small boat sailors, who in any case, presumably have access to charts and maps! Many people still positively enjoy chanting rhythmically 'Belfast, Lisburn, Ballymena, Larne, Carrickfergus, Portrush, Cushendun. Cushendall,' the names of the chief towns in County Antrim in the 1930s and earlier, as they learned them at school, but it is often left to me, an Englishman, to work out travel routes in Ireland!

Many teachers set great store by rote learning especially in memorising multiplication tables, and I would not deny it a place, albeit not a very high one, in educational methods, although new light is cast upon its value by the well-known joke, told to me at a school in Lancashire, by Carl Adams, a boy aged ten, who had a well developed sense of humour. 'A teacher asked a boy to say the two times table, and he began to chant,

' Dah dah de dah,
Dah dah de dah,
Dah dah de dah,
Dah dah'. . . . .

'Stop!' cried the teacher. 'What's the meaning of all this dah, dah de dah nonsense?' 'Sorry sir,' replied the boy, 'I know the tune but I've forgotten the words!'

In cases like that, the tune does not matter and it is the words which count, to say nothing of their meaning, a fact which rote learning often fails to regard. There is however, a difference between learning by rote and learning by heart, as anyone who has learned lines for a play will understand, for no matter how word-perfect the actor is on the night, nearly always, once the play is over, the lines vanish like snow in sunshine, but a poem loved, understood and then repeated, continues to enrich the heart and the mind. Learning by heart is true learning, words, tune and meaning, and is remote from the names of capes and bays.

The assessment of understanding is a subtle process but names and facts can be recited easily, and marks for remembering them can be awarded without difficulty, which may lie behind the earlier importance attached to reeling off long lists of words, for that is all they were, devoid of relevance and meaning. It may also explain Mr Sampson's request that 'poems of literary merit should be memorised,' although he did not resemble the older type of inspector, whom I mentioned earlier. Mr Sampson was pleasant and helpful, but he had been seconded to the inspectorate from the headship of a large public elementary school in a provincial town, and so was aware, from recent experience, of the difficulties and problems of post-War education. He was close to retiring age and was of the old school of teachers in his ideas, but he did not attempt to insist that these should be universal, and recognised that other teachers' opinions might be equally valid.

Throughout my teaching career in Northern Ireland, the annual inspection carried out by a district inspector, who arrived at the school without prior notice, was still the rule, although I understand that this system has now been changed. Mr Sampson called at Kinowla, for his first inspection of my work, in July 1948, when I had been there for six months, and he was reasonably pleased with what he saw. He understood that there was a lot of leeway to be made up, although I felt that he did not appreciate sufficiently the natural reticence of the children, who needed much encouragement to give of their best. His report stated, 'Many children still read and speak in too low a tone,' and so he was unprepared for what he was to hear, a year later, on his second inspection.

For some reason known only to themselves, the Ministry of Education for Northern Ireland did not trust the principals of schools to maintain accurately the statistics of enrolment, attendance etc and so it was one of the Inspector's tasks to check these records, as part of the annual inspection. Neither at that time, did the Ministry trust teachers to supervise the Qualifying Examination in their own schools, and later on, I had to travel 11 miles by taxi to invigilate in another school, yet the actual examination papers were sent to me a week in advance!

It was Mr Sampson's custom to sit at my table checking the figures, while a group of children gathered round the desk to read to him from a book which he had not seen previously. He must have been listening with only half an ear for suddenly he sat up straight in his chair, and abruptly demanded of Pauline Taylor, who was reading to him, 'Why did you shout like that?' Pauline was hurt by this and replied, 'Because in the book it says 'Come here,' he shouted, 'and drop that stick at once!', so I shouted too!' The inspector was taken aback. 'I see,' he said, 'that's very good. You read that very well indeed. Please carry on.'

Emboldened by this, Pauline read on with all the expression which she could muster, and not to be outdone, Nellie Hamilton, who was the next reader, did the same, as did all the others. Mr Sampson abandoned his forms and concentrated upon the children, who evidently pleased him very much, for he complimented them upon the clarity, expressiveness and understanding of their reading. This fine start put him in a good mood, and for the rest of the day everything went well, with the children warming to his praise and doing as well as they possibly could. Neither Mr Sampson nor I could ask for anything better than that, and we were both feeling happy at the end of the school day.

The subsequent report reflected that shared sense of well-being, for it said that there was a particularly pleasant spirit in the senior division, that the children were thoroughly enjoying their school life, and that reading was fluent and distinct, with a good expressive style being cultivated. 'Thank goodness for Pauline Taylor,' I thought, and was certain that the inspection had gone so well because she had given it such an exhilarating beginning: of such little things are good reports made and careers encouraged, for any application for promotion had to be accompanied by copies of the inspector's reports on the work of the school, and great reliance was placed upon them when making appointments. Pauline's enterprise had been instrumental in obtaining such a fine report for our school, and I have always been grateful to her for it, as it was of much help to me in my future career. Yet, as with all examinations, it was not fair that so much credit should be attached to one day's work, which could easily have been as bad as that day's was good, and it was not right that a school should be judged on the happenings of a day's visit. I am told that they order things differently now, and I sincerely hope that 'they' do!

Mr Sampson must have been content with our work at Kinowla, for he did not come again until a year later, when his visit was brief and his report even more brief, devoting just two short approving sentences to educational matters, and two more to the poor condition of the building, which was a welcome new departure. Current inspectors' reports deal almost as much with a school's equipment and buildings as with the education which is carried on there, but no-one reading the earlier reports on Kinowla would have had any idea of the conditions with which the children and staff had to contend; they did not say for example that both classes shared the same room!

It was of course a church school, which meant then, that the rector of the parish was the manager of the school, and had full powers in the appointment of staff, although teachers were paid by the Ministry of Education. The church was responsible for finding 35% of the costs of heating, cleaning and maintaining the fabric of the building, which was an impossible burden for a parish as poor and as small as Kinowla, especially as there were two churches to be maintained, as well as another church school across the border in Skenbarra. All this could not be carried out satisfactorily. The schools were badly neglected as the church buildings had to come first. In the circumstances Brian Davey had no alternative, and I know that he regretted the poor condition of the schools as much as anyone; his own son attended the Skenbarra school, which was even worse than Kinowla. The only way to improve Kinowla School was to transfer it, at least partially, to the County Fermanagh Education Committee, who would then assume complete responsibility for the maintenance of the building. In return for this the management of the school would be in the hands of a committee of six, four representatives of the church and two members from the County Education Committee. Brian was in favour of this as the church would still retain control of the school, but his ecclesiastical superiors refused to accept the change, and the children at Kinowla continued to suffer because of their stubbornness.

Yet change proved to be inevitable, and some time after I left, the school was transferred, and at last a caretaker was appointed. This was the first of many improvements, which culminated in the erection of a new building. In the very long meantime however, the physical and educational health of many children had been impaired, the problems of various rectors of the parish had been increased, and the pitifully small amounts of money which had been spent on the crumbling school buildings, could have been used to better spiritual effect on the work of the two churches. I am not against church schools, but they should be maintained and equipped to the same standards as local authority schools; if this cannot be done then the churches should not retain control, for it is the children who suffer from the poor provision and bad conditions, and their welfare must surely be of paramount importance, otherwise why bother to retain the management of the schools at all?

When I was at Kinowla I found it galling to visit relatively modern, well equipped schools, and to compare them with ours, and it was manifestly unfair that our children should be deprived of many of the things deemed essential for others. Fortunately much has improved since then; many Protestant primary schools have been transferred and on the whole, rural schools are as comfortable and well equipped as any. The present Kinowla School is delightful, and its fortunate 'scholars' have educational opportunities second to none. The role of inspectors in drawing attention to the physical condition of school buildings, and commenting upon equipment, or the lack of it, has been a major factor in bringing about such changes; Mr Sampson's 1950 report was a milestone in the history of Kinowla School.

Mr Sampson was a district inspector, the lowest rank in the inspectorial hierarchy, and he was responsible for the general oversight of schools in a large part of the county; the next rank was senior inspector and above that, staff inspector, such an exalted position, that there were very few of them. The staff inspector for our area was Mr McMillan, known universally as Bertie, and I met him for the first time when he came to Kinowla to discover if I was suitable for recognition as a qualified teacher, at the end of my probationary period of two years. Bertie turned out to be a friendly, seemingly happy-go-lucky character, but there were observant eyes and a sharply analytical mind behind his genial facade.

When he stepped into the room and introduced himself, I felt nervous, for I had guessed the reason for his visit, and was aware of its importance; this feeling of concern persisted throughout the day, despite Bertie's pleasant approach and humorous demeanour. The morning passed peacefully enough and without mishap, and at twelve o'clock the children ate their lunches, and then went out to the field to play, while Mrs Hopkins, Mr McMillan and I gathered round a table for our sandwiches and a cup of tea. Bertie was in expansive mood and when lunch was finished, he lit his pipe, settled in his chair, and obviously at peace with the world, began to tell us about some of his adventures as an inspector.

All too soon, it was time for the children to come in and for work to begin again, but Bertie was in no way ready for this, and went on puffing blue smoke into the air as he recounted more and more tales. I did not know what to do: should I bring the children in promptly and so disturb his mellow mood, or should I leave him to continue enjoying himself? Perhaps it was a trap: in view of all that I had heard about inspectors, it was possible, I thought, that he was testing me, and if I allowed the children to carry on with their play, then he might censure me for not keeping to the correct school hours. From his attitude during the morning however, I was sure that he would not be so devious, so I deferred bringing in the children, and carried on listening to Bertie, although I was unable to devote my full attention to all that he had to say.

At a quarter to one I decided that I must do something, so I moved back my chair and said, 'Well, I suppose I'd better bring in the rascals now, for we're already 15 minutes late.' 'What's the hurry?' replied Bertie. 'Let them stay out and enjoy themselves. It's a fine day isn't it?' and he puffed away in utter contentment. I thought to myself, 'Very well if that's what he wants, I'll not complain.' and Mrs Hopkins made another pot of tea!

It was five past one when the door was flung open violently. 'What's going on?' called a shocked voice. 'Don't you know that it's well after one o'clock and the children are still out playing? Why aren't they in?' and into the room strode Elizabeth, genuinely surprised by our extended break. When she saw our visitor she was quite confused, and much more so when I introduced him to her, but Bertie soon put her at ease, Mrs Hopkins produced another cup, and we all sat there happily until Bertie's pipe went out and he made no attempt to re-fill it.

'Shall I bring them in now?' I asked and when Bertie nodded, I blew the whistle to end the longest lunch-time of my stay at Kinowla. The children eagerly awaited another visit from Mr McMillan, but he never returned to our school; I met him again some years later, and he still recalled my probationary inspection. It lasted for an entire day, and must have been thorough, despite the prolonged lunch break, for I have known the inspection of much larger schools to take only a little longer. A short while after Bertie's visit, came the official letter from the Ministry of Education, 'In view of the favourable nature of the Inspector's report upon your work. . .' etc: my probation was over at long last and I was now a fully fledged teacher, but I didn't feel any different!

The only other visit to Kinowla by an inspector was much shorter than Bertie McMillan's, and turned out to be more of a friendly call than an official occasion. Whilst I was at college in Belfast, Elizabeth and I organised a youth club on the Shankill Road, which was also subject to inspection because it received a grant from the government. One evening we were in the middle of a meeting of the club committee, all of whom

were club members, when a lady came in and introduced
herself as Miss Bell, the Ministry's Inspector of Drama and
Youth Work. I explained what was happening, and she asked
to be allowed to remain in the meeting, so I introduced her to
the young people and we resumed our discussion, just as if she
had not been there, for the members were not at all impressed
by the status of our visitor.

All our meetings were informal, with most of the members
sitting on the floor, in a variety of postures, and only a few on
chairs or stools. No-one at all seemed to be in an orthodox
position, but this gave a feeling of relaxation, and as usual,
ideas flowed freely and the meeting was as lively and uninhibited as ever. Although this had been just a normal meeting, the
inspector was delighted with it, saying that it was all so vital and
fresh, with opinions being given readily, and decisions reached
and accepted: this seemed new to her, but it was just another
meeting to me. Miss Bell came back to the club, and when she
heard that we were moving to Fermanagh, said that she hoped
to call at the school to see the drama work, in which she knew
I was interested.

At that time, neither Miss Bell nor I knew very much about
rural schools, for if we had, there would not have been such talk
about drama work in the school. Nevertheless she kept her
promise and found her way to Kinowla, but with so much
difficulty that, after calling at Carrick Cottage to see Elizabeth,
and only then discovering where the school was, she arrived
there just before the end of the school day, and so was able to
see only a fragment of a play upon which the children were
working. Upon reflection she probably thought herself fortunate to see any drama work at all, for it was not common in
small country schools at that time, and she would have realised
too, that Kinowla was a long way from Shankill Road, and the
outgoing and outspoken young people of that part of West
Belfast were quite unlike the quiet and reserved Fermanagh
children.

Stories of inspectors and schools abound, many of them
doubtless apochryphal, although some of them are so good
that they deserve to be true, and I recall with a smile, an
incident when a visiting inspector asked a boy in my class at
another school, the name of the book which he was reading.

'The Sea Pirates,' said George. Mr Hill misheard him and said, 'The Sea Pilots! I see. What is a pilot?' 'He's a man who drives an aeroplane,' promptly answered George.

'That's right. But what other kind of pilot is there?' The question evoked no response from George or his classmates, until at last a tall ginger-haired boy named Tommy James raised his hand. He was the class joker, always good for a laugh, but his jokes were usually practical ones, since his language skills, although adequate for normal use, were insufficient for amusing byplay with words. 'Please sir, Pontius Pilate,' he said, and looked all around the class, seeking approval for his brainy answer, but they were unimpressed and remained as straight faced as Mr Hill, who quickly explained the role of a maritime pilot, before passing on to other matters, leaving me to enjoy a solitary chuckle at the side of the room. I knew Tommy well enough to understand that the answer had been given perfectly sincerely, with no intention of being thought funny, but the inspector was a serious minded man, and I suspect that he considered that Tommy had been trying to raise a laugh at his expense.

Brian Davey, the rector, came to Kinowla School frequently, and took his duties as its Manager very seriously; at first he taught religious instruction to the senior class once every week although he did not like teaching, but once I had settled in, and he was satisfied with my work, his visits were confined to those of a pastoral nature. He said that he was too impatient to be a good teacher, and certainly this was correct. Although Brian was a learned man, he realised that more than knowledge is needed for successful teaching, but many visitors to classrooms seem unaware of this and cannot impart their skills at all. Some of them, like Brian, recognise their failing, but others do not, and persist in pressing on, to the boredom of the children and the dismay of the teacher.

Some of the clergymen, who descended upon Kinowla School each summer to carry out the annual inspection of religious knowledge, appeared to have little understanding of children, a lack which they shared with their colleagues at diocesan level, who had devised the programme of instruction upon which the examination was based. This consisted chiefly of the study of sections of the Bible, with much emphasis upon the Old Testament, and the catechism and the prayer book; there was much rote learning to be carried out, and little regard was paid to interesting the children in what they had to learn. I often wondered if those responsible for the programme had read over the scriptural passages which they chose for study, as these sometimes contained embarrassing words, phrases and ideas, suitable for discussion with adults, but wildly inappropriate for country children with their sheltered background. To quote one of the least unfortunate examples; when reading the story of Joshua with the class, it was difficult to explain at that time the occupation of Rahab the harlot. Nevertheless, I found that in teaching so much from the Bible, my own Biblical knowledge was increased greatly, and I hope that the same can be said for the children, but I have many doubts about that.

Far too much was expected of them, especially in the portions of the Bible and the Prayer Book which they had to learn for repetition. Most of the children stuck manfully to the task, and if they were not annoyed, I certainly was, when, after committing to memory all the 32 verses of St. Luke, chapter 15, with its parables of the lost sheep, the lost coin and the prodigal son, they were asked at the examination, to say one verse only, and were then marked adversely if they made a slip. When I recalled the time which we had spent in ensuring that as far as possible everyone knew the entire chapter, I was most indignant. If passages from the Bible had to be memorised, it would have been much better to have reduced their length, so that the majesty of the language and its meaning might have been more readily appreciated and understood, and knowledge of the whole section properly tested. As it was, it took so long to hear the children merely recite the complete chapter after learning the various sections, that it was impossible to ensure that they comprehended it fully; for many, of course, even the memorising was beyond them, and I am sure that even those who were able to recite it in full, remember little of it today.

There were many other things to be memorised such as the commandments, the canticles and various psalms and hymns; it was a great struggle and to little real avail. Still it was not without its moments of humour, and I remember Nellie Hamilton reciting confidently and clearly:

'The Son of God goes forth to war
A kingly crown to gain,
His blood-red banner streams afar,
Who follows in THE train.'
I think that the examiner did not notice the mistake!

At least we were spared having to learn off in order, the names of all the books in the Bible, an exercise which was recommended to me because it made it easier to find the various books when they were needed, as if an index had not been invented! The trouble with learning of this kind was that it took up long periods of time which could have been used more beneficially in explanation and discussion, so that the children would have had a much better understanding of what they read during scripture lessons. It was small wonder that, despite Mr Sampson's wish, 'poems of literary merit' were not learned, for enough memorising took place during religious instruction to cover the entire curriculum, and for the most part, the literary merits of the passages being learned could not be disputed, containing as they did, some of the glories of the English language. Yet the sheer drudgery of having to remember so much, tarnished the words and removed all the glory, leaving only the dross of all the wasted labour, to hide the true meaning and value of what had been learned.

It was always a relief when the religious instruction examination was over, for it was such a dull occasion filled with tension and anxiety for the children. They would undoubtedly have welcomed a call from one of the more unorthodox visitors whom we received during the year, although that might have shocked the worthy and reverend gentlemen, whilst giving them a new insight into what really happened in schools!

One day each spring, when leaves were greening the trees, and the cold of winter had gone, a tall, gaunt old woman would appear at the school door. Her face was thin and weather beaten, her hands like gnarled claws with dirt ingrained into their deep creases, and her black clothes never changed. Under a drooping black coat, she wore a long, bedraggled, black frock, which reached down to black stockings and broken black boots, whilst, always the lady, she never appeared without a wide brimmed black hat, which had once been trimmed with artificial flowers, but they had long since vanished.

'Good day to you, Master,' she would say in an old cracked voice, suitable for one of the witches in *Macbeth*, 'It's a fine day today,' as it always was when she called, for she rarely ventured out in bad weather. When I met her for the first time, I made the mistake of lingering at the door with her, and found that she was prepared to chat for ever, although a few pleasant words were not the reason for her visit. After some time listening to her, for she did most of the talking, I became aware that the class behind me was growing restless, so I bade her farewell and turned to go inside.

'Aren't you going to give me something Master?' she asked, and I then realised the purpose of her call. I never had much money in my pocket at school, since I rarely needed any there, but I found a few pennies and gave them to her, whereupon she thanked me profusely and made off quickly down the path. Later on, I learned that she had gone to call on Mrs O'Brien, who was so scared of her, that she allowed her to walk into the kitchen and prepare a fry for herself, without asking any kind of permission, or indeed speaking a word. It must have been weird and unsettling when this dark figure, shambled into the room and silently began to organise a meal for itself, quite impervious to entreaties or threats. It seemed that this was a regular occurrence, and always followed the same disturbing pattern.

After eating, the uninvited guest would sit in the chair beside the fire, making herself comfortable and refusing to leave until she was ready to do so, or until she heard the voices of men in the yard behind the house, whereupon she would gather up her long dress and scamper out of the door and along the road. Beyond this she was a harmless soul, content with a penny or two, except at O'Brien's, where she always cooked herself a meal if the opportunity presented itself. She caused no trouble at the school, where she called twice a year. She was called the 'Fiddler's Woman,' although no-one knew exactly why, for little was known for certain about her. It was thought that she had lived for a time with an itinerant fiddler, who played at weddings and parties, and that either he had left her, or was dead, so that now she was alone. Presumably she had a shelter somewhere for the winter, but as soon as the weather became warmer, she resumed her travels, relying upon meals snatched at houses like O'Brien's, for food, or buying it with the coppers which she was able to beg. The kindly people of Kinowla would willingly have provided her with food, but probably feared that she would then have taken advantage of their generosity and refused to move, or perhaps come back too often. No-one knew where she spent the winter, or where she slept at night, but it was probably in a barn or hay shed somewhere; she came to Kinowla each springtime with the swallows, came back again when the leaves were changing colour, and then vanished until it was spring once more.

At the school she was always polite, and usually waited outside until her knock was answered, but on one occasion I happened to turn round from the group which I was teaching and saw her standing inside the room, looking like a story book witch in her drooping black clothes. I did not recognise her, and as she was obviously frightening the small children near her, I roared 'Get out!' in my surprise at finding such a figure inside the school. Immediately she turned and made off at top speed, holding her hat with one hand and her flapping skirts with the other. She might have been scared at my response, but not out of her wits, for she went straight down to Carrick Cottage, where she informed Elizabeth that I had instructed her to call, and that she was to give her something on my behalf. As this was unusual, Elizabeth thought that there must be some special reason for my request, and gave her more than she would have received from me, so that the 'Fiddler's Woman' departed in excellent spirits, having done very well from her summary ejection from the school.

She was representative of the many itinerant figures who wandered the roads of Fermanagh in those days, before the full development of the welfare state, although I am sure that many of them would have travelled the countryside, no matter how well they were cared for, as they seemed to be unable to remain in any one place for long, and quickly felt the urge to resume their wanderings. Their life was hard, and far from that of the carefree vagabond, beloved of so many romantic poets like Keats and Stevenson, but they apparently preferred their freedom to wander, to the greater comfort of more settled surroundings. Apart from the 'Fiddler's Woman,' few if any of these wanderers called at the school, perhaps remembering their own schooldays (or the lack of them!), or deciding that teachers were not sufficiently affluent to be a soft touch. Any who did call were well received, but none was welcomed as warmly as a group of travelling people, who came to Kinowla School and volunteered to clean our dry toilets. Although I do not know what we would have done without their valuable services, they were paid very little for their unenviable task, and I never knew what they did with the contents, but then, I never asked! To me they were a complete mystery, and I did not know where they came from or where they went, but they carried out an unpleasant job without complaint.

Some of the wanderers were not all that they appeared to be, as I discovered much later in County Tyrone. I had gone home from school for lunch, and Elizabeth told me that she had been visited by a big tramp-like man with an immense beard, who was accompanied by a large, fierce-looking dog. Speaking in an unexpectedly cultured voice, he had asked for directions to Baronscourt, the home of the Duke of Abercorn, which was not a likely destination for such an unconventional figure. Upon hearing that Baronscourt was some 20 miles away, he asked to be directed to the nearest hotel, which was also surprising, for judged by his unkempt looks, the stranger appeared unable to afford the cost of a meal even at the modest hotel in the village. However Elizabeth gave him the necessary directions, for which he thanked her politely and then set off towards the village, with the dog bounding ahead. At school that afternoon there were, most unusually, several absentees, all of whom had failed to return after having gone to their homes in the village for lunch. They all arrived a few minutes later, obviously upset and frightened. When they settled down, they told me that on their way back to school they had seen a big man with a fearsome looking beard, following a giant dog, and they had been so scared that they had run away. They had hidden behind a hedge in a field until the man and his dog had passed by, and even then they had waited for some time before venturing out. The man had neither approached nor spoken to them, but they had been very frightened by his dog.

I did my best to reassure them but to little avail, until on the following Saturday the *Belfast Telegraph* carried an article by Thomas Skelton, the writer and poet, about that week's stage in his walk around Northern Ireland, during which he had called at Baronscourt. His dog, an Irish wolfhound was certainly big enough to scare small children, especially when its master seemed equally terrifying, at least in their imaginations, as they gazed wide-eyed at them, through the hedge behind which they were hiding.

Kinowla was so isolated that we did not receive visits from the entertainers, who in those days, travelled from school to school, giving one-man performances, which included telling jokes, clowning, conjuring tricks, ventriloquism and generally entertaining the children for an hour or so. The admission fee was small but no-one was excluded for being unable to pay, and although the standard was not high, the children always enjoyed the show, laughing heartily at the oldest and feeblest jokes such as 'I call my car Daisy - some days he goes and some days he doesn't!' In a pre-television age such acts were very welcome, and were the only form of live entertainment seen by most rural children, other than local concerts, or performances of the plays of George Shiels, and other 'kitchen comedies,' by Young Farmers' Clubs and similar amateur dramatic societies.

One such entertainer was named Fergie, and he travelled from school to school on a motor bike, with his props, including a live hamster, packed in a box on a carrier over the rear wheel. He would don a bow tie for his performance, and always asked the audience to answer an easy sum or two because he felt that he must include something 'educational' in his act! Many years after the last time I saw Fergie perform, I was most surprised to see a national television programme about him, in which he reminisced nostalgically about his visits to schools, and the warm welcome which he received from children and teachers. He never came to Kinowla, and neither did any other entertainer, for no doubt there were too few schools in the area to make a visit worthwhile, and even those schools had so few pupils that the receipts would not have justified a show. This was a great pity for it would have been well received, despite the age of the jokes and the mediocre quality of the production, and would have been a welcome break in the normal routine of school work.

It is a far cry from the antics of Fergie and his colleagues to the many recitals given by outstanding musicians, both famous and unknown, which I have enjoyed at school during my teaching career. I have taken pleasure in the music, and that pleasure has been increased by the obvious joy and excitement of the young audiences, who, although sitting on hard floors, have been engrossed by the music of Beethoven, Bach, Mozart and many other composers, whose works they had not expected to enjoy. One youthful music critic said to me after a concert given by a chamber ensemble, 'That was better than pop. There's more to it!' yet before the performance she had shown no interest at all, and told me that all she wanted to hear was a pop concert. Similarly I have seen children utterly caught up in plays, in which the cast used no scenery at all, and only basic props and costumes, yet the audiences were completely involved in the action, their imaginations stretched to the full. After one such production a boy said to me, 'They made us think we were really there!,' yet that play had been acted in the middle of a school hall with the children sitting around on the wooden floor. During an 'in the round' version of *Pinocchio,* the children rose to their feet and made it physically impossible for Fox and Cat to capture Pinocchio, who had to leave the hall and make another entry, to enable the story to continue. That was real audience participation, unlike the 'Oh! Yes I can' and 'Oh! No you can't' routines of some circus clowns. Even those would have been welcome at Kinowla, and still more the recitals and plays, for they would have richly fed the hungry imaginations of the children there. With the poverty of their surroundings in the schoolroom, those imaginations needed all the stimuli it was possible to give them, and all our visitors, even the 'Fiddler's Woman' and the book company salesman, were people from the wider world, whose visits might stimulate wonder.

Mrs Hopkins and I worked on alone and we needed the impact of other faces, other minds, other ideas, to supplement our own, and to extend the education which we strove to provide. Each time visitors opened the school door, they let light into the room, but even more important, they opened a door into the minds of the children, lighting up the world beyond the school, relieving some of its mystery, and perhaps, making them wish to know more about it.

11 Goodbye To Kinowla

IT WAS high summer 1950. Rain filled the air as it had for many days, and water was everywhere. The leaves of the trees were studded with raindrops, which showered down to the ground from time to time. Bright beads of water shone in the hedge-rows among the flowers, and when a bird flew through the branches, more water cascaded into the puddles below. The earth was so sodden that when a respite in the rain allowed it to dry for a while, the next downpour saturated it yet again, and water oozed out at the slightest touch.

It had been impossible to cut much of the grass for hay, and the little which had been cut, lay in dank heaps about the fields waiting for the sunshine which never came, for little hay was saved that year. How truly appropriate was that word 'saved,' which the local farmers used to describe hay which had been gathered in, for each year they fought a desperate battle against the elements to make the hay to feed their cattle during the winter. Only when the hay was piled high in sweet-smelling, rounded stacks, had it been saved from the ravages of wind and rain, and another struggle successfully completed. In 1950 however the Kinowla farmers lost their annual tussle in their continuing confrontation with the weather, and the tall blades of grass like hapless victims of the battle, waved their green arms before the conquering storms, or lay down in surrender, surrounded by the brightness of fresh growth, which was already decorated with the glittering insignia of the victorious enemy.

In such conditions, crossing the fields for drinking water was just a hardship, its discomfort even taking away the interest of the variety of wild flowers, which grew among the tall grasses of the hayfields separating Carrick Cottage from the well. Wild orchids were there in profusion and always there were other flowers splashing their colours among the green grass, which grew taller as the weeks of springtime passed. By early summer it almost hid from sight the tip of Oscar's tail, as he forged his way around the edges of the fields, for he had learned quickly not to run through the tall grass in the middle. Sometimes a herd of cattle would be grazing on the rough ground near the well, and then, without a word from me, and with no fuss at all, he would drive them into a line along the opposite hedge whilst I was drawing the water. When I had finished Oscar would glance along the entire line as if to say, 'Don't you dare to move!,' before running back and showing me the way home again. But in high summer 1950 fetching water meant pushing through a jungle of thick grass, knowing that I would be soaked, and there was no pleasure in that. Even Oscar seemed to have lost some of his enthusiasm and he plodded his way almost wearily round the fields instead of bounding along as he usually did.

That year, the normally placid stream, which flowed at the side of the house, was filled with angry water, which, rushing and swirling along, eddied around rocks and splashed wildly against the restraining banks. As the water tumbled and tossed among the stones in its course, the noise of the stream, hitherto heard regularly only in winter, was now our constant companion, so much so that we became hardly aware of it, and noticed its surge only on those rare occasions when the rain eased or stopped altogether, the water level fell, the stream slowed and its menacing roar was silenced.

It was in full voice however, and the rain was falling thickly one late afternoon, when we heard a violent knock at our front door, even louder than the rush of the stream. Outside of the door stood the plump figure of Molly Harvey, the older sister of Hazel and Lily; she wore a wide-brimmed hat, from which a veil of raindrops was dripping, and a long loose coat. Her legs and feet were bare for her shoes were tied together by their laces and were hanging around her neck.

'Master! Master!' she shouted, 'If you don't do something quickly you'll be flooded!,' and when I looked beyond her, I could see that the road was awash with brown water, which was advancing rapidly towards the wall and gate of our house. The stream had broken free from the confinement of its banks, had flowed out across the fields and now unhindered, was fast approaching Carrick Cottage. The road had a high camber but the water had surmounted its rounded crest and soon would be flowing beneath the gate, across the garden and into the house, which was below the level of the road. Down from the gate was a low step, which would soon have made a small waterfall, and as the path sloped downwards, it would not be long before a river would be making its way into the hall. As Molly had said, we had to do something quickly!

Using sods and soil and stone, we built a low barrier across the road to keep the water back and so prevent it from running down into the house. In all this, Molly was an enthusiastic helper; although she had been very wet before she began, she became even wetter as she splashed around in her bare feet, apparently enjoying the opportunity of a paddle away from the seaside, and heedless of the rain and the discomfort. At last the work was finished and the water diverted back across the road and into the stream again. Only then did she resume her long walk home, splashing energetically as she did so, with her hat flopping on her head among a shower of raindrops, and her shoes bobbing up and down around her neck. We watched her walk along the long, straight, empty and very wet road which stretched before her; she strode off into the grey curtain of the rain just as the heroes of Western films rode off into the sunset. As she went we called our renewed thanks to her, at which she turned and waved cheerfully as if she had had a most enjoyable time, like a small child playing with water regardless of any discomfort, but Elizabeth and I went into the house wet, weary and exhausted.

We felt dispirited and disconsolate for this was not the first time we had had to take urgent action to prevent flooding, although the water had never before been so close to the house, and it was then that we decided that we must leave Kinowla. It was not a conscious decision, reached after much discussion and heart searching, but as we looked out upon the drenched fields with the mist enshrouded hills beyond, it seemed that we would be condemned to a perpetual battle against flooding and dampness if we stayed there. Nothing moved except the rain; the hens, ceasing their scratching, had sought silent shelter, and even Oscar, that inveterate optimist, was lying somnolent and listless on the warm straw in his dry outhouse. Only Yorick appeared to be content, for she was stretched idly before the warm glow of the fire, purring comfortably when she could summon the energy to do so, knowing that, despite the rain, for her the living was easy, and that soon she would be fed, without the bother of venturing out into the water-strewn world.

From that time on we knew that we must seek to move, although we had known so much happiness in our cottage, at the school and among our friends, but the rain seemed to circumscribe our future with doubts and hesitations, at least as far as the house with its lack of facilities was concerned. This was high summer indeed, yet we had to have a fire burning in the range to keep the damp at bay; with so much mist and low cloud about, our rooms were dull and sunless; carrying water through wet fields was bearable in winter when it was expected, but not in summer, when it was just a burden; yes we must leave.

There was not another house available in Kinowla, where many people were living in worse conditions than we were, so that an improvement would have to be found elsewhere, although we had no desire to go, other than a wish for a drier house, and perhaps by this time the promptings of ambition. Happy though I was at Kinowla School, I could not see myself staying there for the remainder of my career as a teacher, for I was aware of the increasing developments and rapid changes in education, but felt isolated from them in our remote corner of County Fermanagh, so I began to look for another post.

Fortunately I was soon appointed as the Principal Teacher of a school in County Tyrone, with more pupils and a bigger and better house, but it did not have the warmth and atmosphere of Kinowla. It was situated in a much more prosperous part of the country, an area of fertile land and larger farms, large enough to warrant the employment of farm workers, and so creating social divisions which had hardly existed in Kinowla, where almost all the farms were small enough to be run by the families. The school was centred upon a village, only twelve miles from a large town, where many people went to work each day, and, coming into contact with urban living, urban ideas and urban standards, seemed to lose some of the best qualities of country folk. There was another division, between the villagers and the people who lived away from the village; at school the 'town' children, as they called themselves, tended to regard themselves as more sophisticated than those from the 'country,' although of course, they were all pleasant, unaffected country children.

So too were those at Kinowla, yet the Fermanagh children were more natural, less responsive at first and much more shy, but possessed of a quiet gentleness, an unfeigned friendliness, and a co-operative spirit, which left little room for rivalry and none at all for envy. The lack of division among their elders was reflected in the children, and the greater feeling of tolerance and help so evident at Kinowla among young and old owed a great deal to the lack of social divisions among them. These differences, some real, some imagined, made the village community in County Tyrone, although friendly, more distant than their counterparts in Fermanagh, who were on the whole, less affluent but, probably more content.

Although I was not aware of it at the time, that wet, wet summer of 1950 was to be the cause of great and significant changes all around Kinowla. During those dismal months so much rain had fallen that the turf, cut in the damp bogs in the springtime, and then left in carefully arranged heaps to allow the wind to pass through to dry the blocks of peat, had never dried, and lay out on the hills, sodden and useless. This caused a fuel crisis in many homes, which were without a reserve supply of turf sufficient for many months, and in these, when the peat stack dwindled away, the hearth fire died, the crook and the three legged pots were taken out to a shed to rust away, and beneath the huge chimney open to the sky, a brand new coal-burning range was installed. Instead of a donkey-drawn cart bringing a load of turf from the mountain bog, a coal lorry from Enniskillen delivered fuel to the houses; fires which had burned for many years were finally extinguished, and now, outside only the occasional cottage was the air fragrant with the tang of peat smoke.

This did not happen everywhere of course, for many families were unable to afford to instal a range, and had to eke out their turf until the following year brought new supplies. It did not happen all at once either, but the coming of the range was common enough to herald the arrival of a period of great change in a community which had changed little for generations. From the 1950s onwards, new houses were built in Kinowla village, and with them came a piped water supply to end the burden of water-carrying, and prevent the possibility of water-borne diseases. Although I do not know if any occurred, the danger had been ever present.

The most dramatic agent of change however, was the coming of electricity, for this made possible a host of other changes, the most significant being the advent of television, which was now available to a community which had hardly been aware of the existence of radio. Great changes indeed, and all of them making life less hard for the people of Kinowla, and through television, wider and more interesting. However the impact of the commercial blandishments of the T.V. age posed dangers for people everywhere, many of them much more sophisticated and worldly-wise than Kinowla folk, but I like to think that they were sufficiently wise and stable to 'hold fast to that which is good.' Maybe that is an optimistic hope, for natural, warm-hearted and open country people could possibly be easy prey for the sharp operators of an advertising industry geared to making them think that they must have things without which they have lived happily all their lives. My teaching at Kinowla School would have been very different had the children been accustomed to television, for it would have been a tremendous ally in my bid to widen horizons, but it would have made it more essential to ensure that they appreciated the values of their own traditions, and of the need to maintain them.

In the garden of a house just down the road from where I now live in Northern Ireland, a crane from an old hearth fire has been erected, and from it hang three of the old cooking pots, which in their time must have been used for cooking many things from potatoes to sponge cakes. The crane and the pots have been newly painted in shiny black and are used for growing flowers; the creeping fronds of trailing plants mingle with the bright blossoms of nasturtiums as they twirl their way around the ancient ironwork, just as the blue smoke of the peat fire did in harsher days. Several miles away a water pump, similar to that which once supplied water for the entire population of Kinowla is for sale for £75, not however to provide water for anyone, but as a garden ornament!

As befits its new purpose, it is resplendent in bright blue, quite unlike its workaday counterparts, which were always painted in sober black, and seldom seemed to be newly painted. It is good, if not very appropriate, that these things, which once represented such toil and labour for so many, should now serve as ornaments, for at least this recognises the innate grace and beauty of their simple functional design, yet it would be shameful if they came to be regarded only as decorations and not also as reminders of a way of life which possessed such great strength and dignity as to be well worthy of remembrance.

Rural schools such as Kinowla are important parts of that way of life, and I am sure that as many of them as possible should be retained, not merely out of sentiment or political expediency, but from sheer educational good sense, for these schools prepare their pupils for life as most of them will live it, among their own people in the area where they have been brought up. It is still important to make the children aware of the wider world and to broaden their horizons as I tried to do at Kinowla, but the growth of communications, modern technological developments and the increase in travel opportunities have all made that task easier. In some ways it is now less essential as television has brought fresh aspects of the world into homes everywhere, but even so the guidance of the teacher remains vital to real understanding of what is seen and heard.

The small country primary schools are durable communities, rooted in tradition but not necessarily resistant to change, except that of the fleeting variety, which is of little value anyway. They give country children the chance to begin their education in a calm, settled atmosphere conducive to happiness and true learning, which is more difficult to produce in larger primary schools to which many children have to be transported by bus for quite long distances, and away from their familiar surroundings. Undoubtedly, larger schools often have better facilities, more equipment and other academic advantages, but few personal ones, and in primary schools it is the personal qualities which are all important, for without them, even the very best buildings and the most lavish educational aids are useless in furthering real education. I concede the need for larger schools at the secondary stage, where provision has to be made for the much wider curricular needs of today's children, but I remain convinced of the vital role of the two or three-teacher primary schools in maintaining a stable yet progressive rural population.

The small school is not without its shortcomings however, chief among them being the fact that the children come into contact with so few adults at school. During my time at Kinowla this disadvantage was even greater since nearly all the pupils remained there until they reached the school-leaving age, but re-organisation, and a change of school at the age of eleven, ensured that they then met a greater number and variety of teachers and children, and were offered many more opportunities than the small school could provide.

No doubt even the most remote primary school today receives far more visitors than ever came to Kinowla; peripatetic teachers, advisers, people from the education office and medical staff all come to schools much more frequently than they did, and although this is not an unmixed blessing, they provide contact with the world outside the school walls. Even Kinowla now has ancillary help from welfare and clerical workers, and some schools seek the assistance of parents, so that no longer do most country children meet only two or three adults, during their primary school days. Even so, the teachers are by far the most important, and if for any reason they do not succeed in their task then their pupils will have lost not just one, but several years of their educational lives. The quality of the teachers in our small primary schools is therefore even more vital than it is elsewhere, for their influence is greater than that of their colleagues in larger primary schools, where contact with individual children is more restricted, and lasts for a much shorter time.

The training of teachers for country schools is also important since it requires special techniques to teach a class consisting of children of such wide age and ability ranges. Many teachers who have taught only classes arranged according to chronological age, might find it difficult to understand how to teach a class of 25 boys and girls aged from 9-14, as I did at Kinowla, or the class of 40 or more of a similar age-range, which I taught in Co. Tyrone. It is by no means the same task as taking a group of 30-35 children all of similar ages, and so I was surprised that when I was at college, no time at all was spent in preparing students for teaching in rural schools, although there are so many of these all over Northern Ireland.

There came a time however when the value of such schools began to be questioned, and it became fashionable and economically expedient to suggest that many of them should be closed and amalgamated with others to form bigger ones. There appeared to be little consultation with teachers about this idea, but what would now be termed, rather grandly, in-service training courses were organised to discuss methods suitable for use in such larger establishments. I went to one of these courses with a friend who was also the principal of a two teacher school, and at the end of the day he was fuming with indignation. 'Here they are,' he exclaimed, 'wanting to close small schools, and yet they are encouraging the use of the very methods which we have always used in them!'

This was very true, for the lecturers at the course were advocating the wisdom and effectiveness of the individual and group teaching which was carried out in all small schools, as opposed to the teaching of the entire class as a single unit, which was often done in large schools. Still it was only at such courses that I heard these matters discussed at all, even though it was not in the context of small schools; for most of us who went to teach in them, it was a matter of learning as we went along, in my case with the help of the children of Kinowla! We found it far from ideal however and most teachers in small schools, at some time in their careers, must have longed for the apparent simplicity of one age-group - one class, although this simplicity is an illusion for it means merely a different set of problems and not an end to them!

The small rural school is a valuable institution for country areas where numbers are not high and the population is a steady one with much experience of the kind of education which it provides. However, to attempt to use its methods in urban areas with bigger classes does not always lead to the success which they have known elsewhere, where circumstances and conditions are very different. Apparently choosing to ignore this, and without carrying out any research to support their theory, some educationists suggested that school classes should no longer consist of children of the same age, but should contain entire families, no matter how different their ages or abilities. Teachers must surely possess a masochistic streak, for many of them went along with this idea, which was called 'family grouping,' but when in spite of all their efforts it was unsuccessful, the name was changed to 'vertical grouping,' and classes were formed, not with families, but with children aged from 4-7, and from 7-11 as in country schools. Such arrangements were convenient administratively as they helped to reduce the numbers of teachers required, since the mixed age-group classes were as large as their predecessors, and it was assumed that because small schools worked such a system effectively, it could easily be done anywhere.

In 1968 I was appointed headmaster of a large new urban primary school in the north of England, which was officially opened by the principal of a well known college of education. She was most surprised that the school was organised along traditional lines instead of having the then fashionable vertically grouped classes, and her surprise was even greater when I told her that I had been the principal teacher of two rural schools where such grouping had been inevitable. Although she had had no practical experience of such arrangements, she was convinced that they must work well, and failed to appreciate that if teaching 35 children of the same age is not easy, then it must be even more troublesome to teach 35 aged from 7-11, or even 7-9 or 9-11. Yet masochists as they are many teachers tried to work in this way-a self inflicted punishment indeed! By now, however, the vogue for vertical grouping has faded, and little is heard of the system today, except where it is thrust upon teachers by falling numbers, and then it is recognised as educationally unsound, and an expedient to be avoided if at all possible, even by those who seek to solve problems on paper and not in the classroom.

I returned to Kinowla Primary School several times after I had left my post as principal teacher there, but not until November 1983 was I able to visit the school at work for I had always called there during our holidays from school. There is now no trace of the old building which I knew so well, and in its place is a new brick-built school with a professionally made name board. At the front is a car park and two well kept lawns, whilst at the back is a triangular shaped field, still recognisable as the football and handball pitch, but well grassed and devoid of rushes, although it is much smaller than I remember.

Inside there are three amply sized rooms, two used for classrooms, and the other, the largest of the three, as a hall for dining, P. E. and other activities which require much space. The rooms have large windows, and are well lit and comfortably furnished, cluttered with the usual impedimenta of the classroom but uncrowded, and apparently well equipped with books and materials. There is a piano and a colour television set, which made me recall ruefully that at my last new school in England, which had been built several years later than the new Kinowla School, we had had to be content with a black and white one! There is also an excellent radio, much better than my wee blue portable set!

At the time of my visit the walls were bright with colourful pictures and patterns, which had been painted by most of the children in the school, whose art work was obviously much better and much more attractive than that of my pupils over 30 years before. The present head teacher pointed out, however, that many of my children would have painted very little, if at all, at school before the provision of free materials in 1948, and few of them would have had even coloured pencils at home, so that they would have been inexperienced in art work compared with her present day charges; a tactful and encouraging remark, which help to assuage my embarrassment when I recalled the daubs of Pauline Taylor.

In 1983 there were two teachers and 22 children at the school, the smallest enrolment ever, but the principal thought that numbers would increase, a forecast which proved to be correct, for Kinowla Primary School now has 34 pupils, sufficient to ensure that it will remain open for some time to come. As I had expected the girls and boys at Kinowla were delightful: more immediately responsive and open than their predecessors, and less shy although certainly not forward. They were happy and content, although one boy informed me that he did not like school at all, and could hardly wait to be old enough to start work on a farm! The fact that he felt free to say this so frankly to a stranger, said much for his teachers and for the open atmosphere and honest attitudes which they had engendered among their pupils. Only one family walked to school and the others came on the bus or were brought to the school by their parents in cars. . . 'Wee Hughie', who was taken by the hand, has long since vanished!

As I looked at the children at the school, sitting informally around me and conversing freely, I was impressed by their appearance, for they were all warm, comfortable, at ease and very well clad, with 'shining morning faces' still, although the school day was almost over, a sharp contrast to the children in the 1948 photograph, some of whom looked cold and not too well dressed, as they gazed at the camera on that dull February day so long ago. The new school had opened in 1967 and with it had come the improvement in conditions, which had been denied to Kinowla children for generations, and which had clearly done so much for them, not only physically, but socially and educationally as well.

With the building of the new school and the coming of secondary education, albeit on a selective basis, opportunities now exist for all the children, with those who do not pass the 11+ examination, able to attend a High School in Enniskillen, and so no longer compelled to remain at Kinowla, which could never give them a secondary education fitting for modern needs, although its record as a primary school is good. In the words of one of Mr Sampson's early reports, 'the children are making the progress of which each is capable', and obviously the same remarks apply today.

It is true that although numbers have increased, they remain low; the teachers are fortunate in having small classes, and the pupils are fortunate also in being taught in such good conditions, but it is right that at long last, the children of Kinowla should be so well favoured, for they had been educationally deprived for such a long, long time. No doubt the school is costly to maintain, and a case for closing it on economic grounds could be made, but it will take many years to make up for the money which was saved for so long at the expense of so many children. After all, they had to endure conditions which would have been accounted sub-standard even at the turn of the century, and if the present pupils of Kinowla School seem to be receiving a little more than their share of the educational cake, then that is some recompense for the long time when their forebears received little more than crumbs. I cannot recall ever hearing any of the children at Kinowla complain, for they appeared to be unaware of their educational deprivations and were content to make what they could of the little which was given to them. It would be cruel and ironic if after all that, and when its conditions are as good as those of any school anywhere, the new Kinowla School, with all its excellencies, should after such a short life, have to close because of lack of numbers, when the old school, ramshackle and ill-equipped as it was, served the community for so long. At least for the time being that danger has receded, and I hope that there will be a school at Kinowla to serve many generations yet to come.

The photograph is discoloured and holds those Kinowla children in a poor light, but I see them in the brightness of a film of memory projected so far down the tunnel of the years, that the picture is small, but all the more sharp and clearly focussed for that. They smile or stare or shiver or merely stand impassively but I recall them in all their moods, a changing kaleidoscope of emotions, which coalesces into a rounded, glowing warmth of happiness and contentment, bringing to me in turn feelings of pleasure and satisfaction at having known and worked among them. Perhaps I gaze at them across the years with too much nostalgia, maybe my memory is selective, for I am fully aware that life at Kinowla was not always unclouded. I know that any bright light must cast a shadow, yet I am certain that the time I spent there, short though it was, was the most fulfilling and the most rewarding of all my teaching career. I did not think so at the time, and I remember being troubled often with doubts and a sense of frustration and failure, but in spite of that, it is to Kinowla that my thoughts return when I seek any sense of achievement from my years of teaching. Of all the children I have known during those years, I remember best those of Kinowla, quiet, friendly and helpful, who did so much to help me to grow as a teacher, and whose memory is still so bright to me today. I hope that I helped them also, and that their memories of Kinowla Public Elementary School are as pleasant and enduring as mine.

Also available

FERMANAGH CHILDHOOD

BY WILLIAM K. PARKE

A best selling book about village life fifty years ago. Willie Parke writes with remarkable clarity about a time when the village was the hub of social and economic activities for the surrounding countryside and its farming community. It was also a time of change and contrast between the wars, when the village had a limited electricity supply but no running water; when tractors and lorries were making their first appearance, but there was still general reliance on the horse.

The book describes school life and the pastimes of the children, the characters they met and their fascination with the bustling life around them. They watched the blacksmith at his forge, held the horses outside the creamery, cared for the animals, and in Willie's case helped in the family shop, the centre of the local universe.

£4.50
ISBN 0 946872 02 0

AND THE BAND PLAYED ON
Sketches of Ulster life

BY GERRY RAFFERTY

This book is a series of brief stories about life in Armagh in the thirties and forties. It is light and humorous in style, but is a mine of information about a way of life now gone, highlighting childhood, shopping, leisure activities, local trades and occupations, agricultural practices and the characters of a rural area.

The stories, written by a popular local journalist and native of Armagh, are rich and varied. They tell of Sam's shop where shawled women came in for their paper poke of Gallagher's snuff; cutting pea rods for the master; potato picking and apple pulling; and people such as the oil cloth man and the steam roller man who covered the country.

On the leisure side, Gerry Rafferty recounts tales of the tin dance halls and nights at the Cosy Corner Picture House and the famous Armagh bullet throwers with their unique game of road bowls.

£4.95
ISBN 0 946872 37 6

POST 381
The memoirs of a Belfast air raid warden

BY JAMES DOHERTY

James Doherty grew up in North Belfast and was just starting out on his working career at the outbreak of the second world war. He volunteered to become an air raid warden, part of the civil defence of his city.

This book is a compelling eye witness account of the dramatic scenes in 1941 when Belfast came under devastating attack. The author was actively involved in many aspects of the blitz. His home was destroyed, he helped to rescue survivors, volunteered for duty at the makeshift morgue at the Falls Road baths and worked with his civil defence colleagues to cope with the problems of the homeless.

Post 381 is a record of civil defence in Belfast during the war and a moving account of the hardship suffered on the home front. It describes with affection a way of life which has changed for ever; the passing of an era.

£4.95
ISBN 0 946872 27 9